GHETTO SOCIAL STRUCTURE: A SURVEY OF
BLACK BOSTONIANS

Joe R. Feagin

University of Texas at Austin

Printed in 1974 by

R AND E RESEARCH ASSOCIATES
4843 Mission Street, San Francisco 94112
18581 McFarland Avenue, Saratoga, California 95070

Publishers and Distributors of Ethnic Studies
Editor: Adam S. Eterovich
Publisher: Robert D. Reed

Library of Congress Card Catalog Number

74-21138

ISBN

0-88247-308-5

PREFACE

This book is a revised version of my Harvard Ph.D. dissertation entitled The Social Ties of Negroes in an Urban Environment (1966). In preparing the dissertation for publication I have made numerous editorial changes, but because of time and space limitations I have not undertaken a thorough revision of the literature discussion or an expansion of the data analysis. Surprisingly, and unfortunately, little empirical or survey research on the social structure of ghetto communities has been conducted since 1966; most of the further research proposed in this monograph remains to be done. Those readers interested in an updated review of the literature on the social structure of black communities may refer to David Perry and Joe Feagin, "Stereotyping in Black and White," in People and Politics in Urban Society, edited by H. Hahn (Beverly Hills: Sage, 1972), pp. 433-463.[1] Those readers interested in the final research report on the larger Boston Housing Study, the research study from which the data in this monograph were taken, may refer to Joe Feagin, Charles Tilly, and Constance Williams, Subsidizing the Poor (Boston: D. C. Heath and Co., 1972). Bibliographical references to the low-income housing literature will be found in this latter volume.

Most of the data analyzed in this monograph were obtained through my participation in an evaluation study of a low-income housing demonstration project carried out by the Boston Housing Authority and financed by the Low-Income Housing Demonstration Program in what is now the U. S. Department of Housing and Urban Development (HUD). I am grateful to Mr. George B. Nesbitt of the Low-Income Housing Demonstration Program and Mr. Ellis Ash of the Boston Housing Authority for permission to use in this monograph some of the interview results from that evaluation study.

I am also indebted to the Social Science Quarterly, Social Forces, and the International Journal of Contemporary Sociology for permission to publish here the original chapters on which articles for those journals were based.[2]

I would particularly like to acknowledge the wise guidance and counsel of Charles Tilly, my Ph.D. dissertation adivser, and of Thomas F. Pettigrew and Harrison White in shaping the original research plan behind this monograph. And I would like to thank my wife, Clairece Booher Feagin, and Nancy Becker, for their gracious typing assistance, without which this monograph would never have been published.[3]

---

[1]Two recent studies not included in that review might also be noted: William C. Hays and Charles H. Mindel, "Extended Kinship Relations in Black and White Families," Journal of Marriage and the Family, 35 (February, 1973), 51-57; Marvin Olsen, "Social and Political Participation of Blacks," American Sociological Review, 35 (August, 1970), 682-697. A few general studies are also of relevance to the comprehensive study of social organization in black communities, such as Gerald Suttles, The Social Order of the Slum (Chicago: University of Chicago Press, 1968).

[2] Joe R. Feagin, "The Kinship Ties of Negro Urbanites," Social Science Quarterly, 49 (1968), 660-665; Joe R. Feagin, "A Note on the Friendship Ties of Black Urbanites," Social Forces, 49 (1970), 303-308; Joe R. Feagin "Social Organization of the Black Ghetto," International Journal of Contemporary Sociology, 9 (1972), 108-116.

[3] I am also greatly indebted to the dedicated research staff of the Boston Housing Study.

TABLE OF CONTENTS

LIST OF TABLES

LIST OF FIGURES

CHAPTER I

SOCIAL ORGANIZATION IN THE BLACK GHETTO

For several decades now obituary notices concerning the demise of personal
social ties in modern urban communities have been appearing in the writings of
some sociologists and other social scientists. Certain classical sociologists,
such as Louis Wirth and Georg Simmel, some time ago presented a picture of urban
anonymity and the absence of binding social ties, beyond the formal association
level, for urban dwellers. In a famous essay, "Urbanism as a Way of Life," Louis
Wirth set forth a number of identifying characteristics of the city, such as
density and heterogeneity, and the impact that such factors have had upon the
social ties of urbanites.[1] In this very influential statement of his position
he argues that the emerging urban way of life, more particularly the urban social
way of life, is characterized by

> ...the substitution of secondary for primary contacts, the
> weakening of bonds of kinship, and the declining social
> significance of the family, the disappearance of the neighborhood,
> and the undermining of the traditional basis of social solidarity.[2]

Contemporary writers on community life and urban society have absorbed
these rather specific ideas about urbanization and have perpetuated them in
sometimes more subtle, sometimes more grandiose, forms. In a recent book
dealing with studies of American community life, Maurice Stein takes a
neo-Wirthian position on the effects of urbanization.[3] He argues that urbanization has been essentially a disorganizing force and that most modern
urbanites are caught up in an impersonal world of intense competition and
interpersonal manipulation. Depersonalizing trends have transformed personal
social relationships into object relationships valued only as sources of
status and material reward. As individuals have become increasingly dependent
upon impersonal bureaucracies and formal organizations, personal loyalties,
such as neighborhood and family ties, have generally declined or disappeared.
Alienation and anomie predominate in "our huge impersonal cities, where most
human encounters are mediated by superficial amenities."[4]

This neo-Wirthian theme of the "eclipse of community," of isolation,
impersonality, and disorganization, has also stayed with us in the more
general literature bemoaning the alienation and anomie of modern urban
civilization. Herbert Marcuse, in effect, believes that Orwell's 1984
has already arrived. Centralized authorities and impersonal manipulators,
such as mass media administrators, have already replaced traditional social
controls, presumably those controls once furnished by the late lamented
kinship, friendship, and local community ties. The removal of these pernicious
centralized authorities would only "plunge the individual into a traumatic void."[5]

Arguing in a similar vein, Robert A. Nisbet views with alarm the decline of intimate personal ties in an increasingly urban society. He argues that "alienation from place and property turns out to be, at bottom, estrangement from close personal ties which give lasting identity to each."[6] He also notes an intense "quest for community," a quest which has succeeded only in the formation of "pseudo-intimacy" with others, a pathetic reliance on superficial symbols of friendship and association furnished by Hollywood and the other mass media. In general, Nisbet sees contemporary urbanites as a mass of insecure, lonely, and unattached individuals, whose ordinary social relationships -- where they do exist -- are devoid of psychological meaning. The social ties generated under the umbrella of bureaucratic authority and impersonal formal organizations are devoid of effective meaning and cannot replace the loss of "small social and local groups within which the cravings for psychological security and identification could be satisfied."[7] These themes of impersonality, anonymity, and disorganization can also be found as undercurrents in writings in other areas,[8] but the aforementioned studies should suffice to show how subtle, and not-so-subtle, versions of Wirth's original position have remained with us in the general literature on community life and urban society.

Other students of community life and urban society have challenged this general point of view, presenting general evidence for the extensiveness of primary group life in all urban areas, including substantial evidence for the persistence of neighboring patterns, kinship networks, friendship cliques, and family life. In addition, recent studies of voluntary association memberships of Americans have indicated that a majority belong to no secondary organizations except, perhaps, a church; even formal work settings seem to be conducive to primary group behavior, such as friendship and cliques. Extensive documentation for these points can be found in Greer, Bell and Boat, and Hausknecht, among others, and will not be elaborated here.[9]

Wirth-like arguments about urbanization and urbanism have also had a heavy influence on views of slum and ghetto subcommunities within urban complexes. Some researchers have seen the slum as accentuating the worst features of urban life, particularly its isolation, anonymity, and social disorganization. Burgess and his fellow ecologists early adopted a view of the city as a series of concentric circles or zones.[10] Zone I, encompassing the central business district of the city, is surrounded by a zone of transition; this zone of transition is the slag heap of urban society, characterized by deteriorated housing, high juvenile delinquency rates, high morbidity, and excessive crime. This picture of social disorganization in the zone of transition was substantiated in the studies of Shaw and Zorbaugh.[11] In his classical study of Chicago's North Side, Zorbaugh found an area of anomie, isolated urban dwellers, and social disorganization.[12] R. D. McKenzie's comments indicate the tone of much of the early thinking about social structure in the slum:

Slums have been characterized as "areas of lost souls and missions," areas where individuals and family groups are living in enforced intimacy with people whom they naturally shun and avoid; areas where there are no standards of decency or social conduct except those imposed by outside authority. In such an environment the individual has no status, there is no representative citizen, the human desires for recognition and security remain unsatisfied.[13]

C. C. North has argued in similar fashion that the lower socioeconomic brackets operate within a sphere of mental isolation and preoccupation with "the more trivial interests of life."[14] Knupfer brings some data to bear on this question and argues that lower status persons are quite limited in face-to-face contacts. "Informal social activities, such as visiting friends, are more infrequent among them."[15] She concludes that low status produces a lack of interest in social activities, formal and informal; a concomitant lack of self-confidence results in a withdrawal from participation in these social areas and a greater dependence on the mass media for their ties to the community. Even today one finds that some urban renewal administrators and their Chamber of Commerce propagandists, arguing for the demolition of slum areas, emphasize their anonymity, juvenile delinquency, and crime, as Gans suggests in his discussion of urban renewal in Boston's West End.[16]

Although somewhat less influential, another view of the slum is radically different. Some time ago William F. Whyte raised some very serious doubts about the general view of the slum as an urban jungle.[17] He argued that the Chicago sociologists, such as Burgess and Zorbaugh, based their speculations about the slum on ad hoc impressions rather than upon systematic observation. His own procedure was to do a participant observation study in a slum area; it was an underlying impulse of Street Corner Society to show that extensive social organization does exist in the slum.[18] Whyte did not find an urban jungle, but a well-organized slum area. On the basis of his own research he further argues that there are different types of slum areas, ranging from highly individualized rooming-house districts to highly organized immigrant ghettos. A recent study of Boston's West End was motivated by a purpose similar to that of Whyte: to show the extent of organization in an area termed "blighted" and destined for slum clearance. Participant observation in the West End revealed to Gans an "urban village," populated by Italian immigrants adapting their institutions to urban life.[19] Gans concludes that

> the basis of adult West End life is peer group sociability.... West Enders live within the group; they do not like to be alone. Thus, what has been noted earlier about teenagers -- that they are quiet and passive by themselves and burst into activity only with their peers -- is true almost as much among adults. Indeed, for most West Enders, people who have been trained from childhood to function solely within the group, being alone brings discomfort and ultimately fear. The discomfort was expressed by housewives who got their housework done quickly so as to be able "to visit."[20]

For some people the West End had all the earmarks of a slum: old, somewhat deteriorated, some fire hazards, a low-rent area housing a heterogeneous collection of poor people. But Gans emphasized that one must distinguish between a low-rent area which is an urban village, that is, which is poor but proud and organized, and an urban jungle which is poor and disorganized. In like manner, students of other ethnic slums, such as Jewish ghettos, have emphasized the intimate kinship and friendship ties which proliferate within a low-status area encapsulated by law and custom.[21] These two radically different views of the slum can be summarized as follows: (1) one sees the slum as a jungle, emphasizing the worst features of Wirth's picture of urban life; and (2) the other sees the slum as a village, emphasizing the intimate social ties among its residents and usually distinguishing an ethnic slum, or ghetto, from other slum areas.

At a time when some are beginning to look beyond the social pathology of ethnic (white) slum life to its social organization, others are still writing one-sided accounts of the black ghetto. Some time ago in <u>An American Dilemma</u> Myrdal argued that the characteristic traits of the Negro community were forms of social pathology: the unstable, black family, the insufficient recreational activities, the narrowness of interests of the average black American. Even the social organization which he did find, "the plethora of Negro sociable organizations," was viewed as little more than a pathological reaction to caste pressures.[22] Some recent students of the black ghettos have not modified this view of the ghetto as institutionalized pathology. Kenneth Clark in his book on Harlem contends that

> the dark ghetto is institutionalized pathology; it is chronic, self-perpetuating pathology; and it is a futile attempt of those with power to confine that pathology so as to prevent the spread of its contagion to the larger community. It would follow that one would find in the ghetto such symptoms of social disorgani- zation and disease as high rates of juvenile delinquency, veneral disease among young people, narcotic addiction, illegitimacy, homocide, and suicide.[23]

And he comments on the established and sect churches:

> Established Negro churches, the many storefront churches and the sporadic Negro quasireligious cult groups, like Father Divine's and the late Daddy Grace's followers, play chiefly a cathartic role for the Negro.[24]

Partially influenced by this Harlem study, a recent federal government report, <u>The Negro Family: the Case for National Action</u>, moves in <u>non sequitur</u> fashion from an analysis of the family instability of a minority of families within black ghettos to a description of the whole black community as disorganized and in a state of "massive deterioration."[25] It seems that the authors of this report, along with others, let the disorganization of a minority obscure their view of the organization of the majority. One-quarter of black families may be "broken," but the other three-quarters are intact. Certainly family problems, as well as other types of social problems, do exist to a dispropor- tionate degree in black ghettos. But surely it is an exterme exaggeration to state as a matter of fact that

> to those living in the heart of a ghetto, black comes to mean not just "stay back," but also membership in a community of persons who think poorly of each other, who manipulate each other, who give each other small comfort in a desperate world.[26]

Such views of life in a black ghetto seem one-sided and overstated. They tend to depict the whole of ghetto life as nothing more than a pathological reaction to white segregation and discrimination. This distortion overlooks important organizational aspects of a black community. Are there no unbroken homes in a ghetto? No ordinary friendships? No functioning kinship networks? Could it be that for a hundred years Negroes have only been reacting? Does not ordinary social life exist, even in a poor black ghetto, for a majority of the residents?

An adequate answer to this latter question would be critical for several reasons. In the first place, such an answer would help correct the "ghetto as disorganization" image usually applied to black areas. Of the two radically different views of the slum in the literature the "slum as jungle" has usually been applied to black ghettos, while the "slum as village" has generally not been used in regard to these same ghettos. In the second place, certain research evidence suggests that existing social organization within a black ghetto may be useful in explaining, in part at least, non-migration phenomena. A recent study of the Boston ghetto revealed that most of a group of middle-income families who could afford to move out of the ghetto had not seriously explored the possibility.[27] Just when some good housing is becoming available for Negroes in certain areas of Boston, many of them expressed unexpected reticence toward leaving the ghetto.[28]

In 1965 I interviewed twenty black "leaders" in the Boston ghetto, probing for their thoughts on the general housing situation in Boston.[29] Some of them gave explanations of this non-migration phenomenon which further suggested the importance of systematically studying the social ties of a representative group of ghetto families. In addition to the expected explanations of fear of discrimination and vested interest, I was surprised that half of the leaders who gave explanations for the non-migration gave answers largely in terms of social ties. Some answers to the question fell into the general category of "attachment to the community." One of the black politicians put it this way:

> I don't see how Roxbury can become desegregated. People like to live in this area. Some Negroes have even been making complaints about the whites in 221(d)3 projects taking the place of Negroes who are site tenants.

The past president of a civil rights organization, adamant about the right of blacks to move out of the ghetto, still felt that

> Negroes like where they are living. It is the individual Negro's prerogative to move. Plenty of Negroes are moving out -- to places like Randolph. But people like me don't want to move anyplace. My daughter has decided to live nearby because of transportation and the quality of the housing. But the masses (sic) of Negroes don't want to move. They stay where their roots are.

This last metaphor was used by several leaders with whom I talked; one young civil rights leader, a militant who sees herself as a leader of lower-class blacks, said that she wants her child "to have roots," this being given as one of the reasons why she never intends to move out of the Roxbury area.

Proximity, either of mother and child or friend and friend, results more often than not in continued proximity. Coupled with this proximity is the accumulation of shared experiences, opinions, and values. The growth of such sharing and communication increases the cohesiveness of the social force between two or more units. One of the forces which keeps blacks (who are potentially able to move) in the Roxbury area may well be the same as that which tends to keep East Boston predominantly Italian and South Boston substantially Irish: intimate kinship and friendship networks. "All my friends," concluded a newspaperman, "live in the ghetto." He went on:

Some young collegiates with fewer attachments are moving out to
the suburbs. The strongest ties to the ghetto are friends and
relatives. Relative ties are strong on a relative basis, and
also on a race basis. There is strength in such bunches.

In response to a probe on what brings migrants to Boston, he further
suggested that "migrants come to Boston mostly because of friends and
relatives. But, if I were in Detroit, I would say they mostly came because
of work." Others, including leaders of lower-class (oriented) organizations, did
mention in discussing the question of why they personally would not move,
their fear of breaking community ties, of being out of touch with their friends,
and of having to commute to see their relatives and attend organizational functions.

Admittedly, other major reasons for this reticence to move were suggested
by the leaders. Several mentioned the vested interest of Negro businessmen,
professionals, and politicians; a certain preference for "urbanity" was also
suggested as a reason, that is, preference for easy transportation, for the
bustle of life in the city, for the night life and entertainment facilities.
Nevertheless, the comments which leaders made to me in these unstructured
interviews -- at the very least -- suggest that it is time that positive
social forces in urban ghettos were systematically investigated.

Although there has been a general failure to study systematically these
positive social forces within black communities, some studies in the area
of race relations have touched, usually indirectly, upon the social contacts
of blacks. The direct concern of most of the studies has been with interracial
contacts. One large group of studies have focussed upon discrimination in
rather small, and usually southern, towns. For example, one classic study,
Deep South, primarily deals with the interracial contact patterns and segregation of a Mississippi town;[30] other typical studies, such as Caste and Class
in a Southern Town and After Freedom, deal similarly with caste patterns in
education, politics, and religion.[31] Each of these three studies does spend
some time examining the internal class structure of small southern towns.
Only Deep South goes into any detail on the social contacts and cliques of
some of the black residents; and this analysis of cliques is hampered by its
being used primarily as a tool for the analysis of class differentiation.

Studies of black communities in large urban areas also concentrate
on interracial contacts, segregation, and social disorganization; two works,
Dark Ghetto[32] and Beyond the Melting Pot,[33] focus on discrimination patterns
in Harlem's job, housing, and school arenas, the former emphasizing its
essential pathology and the latter its lack of internal community organization.
Partial exceptions to the preoccupation with discrimination and disorganization can be noted. St. Clair Drake and Horace Cayton in their classic study
of Negro life in Chicago have given us a significant glimpse into the class
system of a northern, urban community.[34] Although they are primarily concerned
with the history of segregation, its contemporary patterns, and class structure
in Chicago, they also mention the organizational life of Negro urbanites.
More will be said about their view of black associational life in a later chapter.
Following their lead, Babchuk and Thompson have completed the only systematic
study of the voluntary associational memberships of blacks.[35] And Meadow,[36]
although primarily concerned with black-white differences, has reported some
data on the informal social ties of blacks in Detroit. Thus Meadow and
Babchuk do provide some data on the social ties of blacks in urban ghettos,
data which will be used in later chapters for comparative purposes. Certain

studies of housing and migration, although only indirectly concerned with the internal integration of the black community, can also be milked for some useful comparative data.[37] In general, as of the mid-1960's, it appears that there has been a preoccupation in the race relations literature with discrimination against blacks and disorganization or pathology within black ghettos. At a time when it has become fashionable to discuss the disorganization of urban black communities, we have to admit that we know   little about the ordinary social organization and social integration of those same communities; that is, few have systematically investigated the integration of black families into the urban social fabric.

In the literature of the social sciences one can find several different meanings given to the term "social integration." In the field of race relations it is often synonymous with racial integration, the bringing of black Americans into positions of equal status with whites in American society. This is not the sense in which I am using the term. In a suggestive theoretical paper Werner Landecker specifically answers the question "What is integration?" and attempts to suggest how social integration might be measured.[38] He suggests four types of integration: cultural, normative, functional, and communicative. "Cultural integration" refers to the degree of consistency or inconsistency among the standards of a culture, while "normative integration" relates to the degree of conformity of individuals to these cultural standards. "Functional integration" is integration in the sense of economic interdependence and division of labor. More pertinent to my purpose here is Landecker's conception of "communicative integration." This type of social integration concerns the way in which people are integrated in relation to one another, that is, the extent of interpersonal interaction. One quantitative index of communicative integration, Landecker suggests, would be the percentage of the members of a particular group who are in social isolation.

The importance of interpersonal interaction, or communicative integration, has been emphasized by Lazarsfeld and Katz:

> Interpersonal relations seem to be "anchorage" points for
> individual opinions, attitudes, habits and values. That is,
> interacting individuals seem collectively and continuously
> to generate and to maintain common ideas and behavior patterns
> which they are reluctant to surrender or to modify unilaterally.[39]

They go on to assess the significance of small, intimate groups in terms of the intervening role they play in the influence process; small group intervention between the mass media and the individual is of central concern. Their survey of extant research substantially supports the importance of communicative integration in urban social life; communications do proceed along informal interpersonal networks. Opinions are anchored in such networks. Communication between individuals and families need not be construed only in terms of messages, opinions, or "news." Broadly conceived, communication can be seen as including the exchange of help, money, and aid between relatives or friends, the exchange of marriage partners between families which have for a long time been friends, or the exchange of job favors between relatives or friends. And, in socio-psychological terms, interpersonal relations often provide for the exchange of affectual support and emotional security.

Conclusion

The general neglect of social organization within black ghettos strongly suggests the need for an intensive examination of this organization, including interpersonal relations in both formal and informal settings. The "jungle" image of the slum has, as noted earlier, been criticized by several researchers, although it is still the prevailing image of the black ghetto. To offset this undue emphasis on social disorganization, this monograph will investigate the extent to which urban black residents maintain interpersonal ties, even within the Boston ghetto. Landecker, Lazarsfeld, and Katz -- among others -- suggest the profound significance of interpersonal relations as anchorage points for individual attitudes, habits, and values and as media for the exchange of those important communications which provide the cohesiveness of the urban social fabric. It is the general premise of this report that interpersonal relationships are of the same basic significance for black Americans as they are for other urban residents, including those living in other racial-ethnic "slums." The specific indices of interpersonal relationships which will be used in this report are as follows: (1) the extent, intensity, and sources of friendship contacts; (2) the extent and intensity of neighboring; and (3) the extent and intensity of kinship contacts. Two further types of social participation will be examined in order to give a fuller picture of the social integration of these black families: (1) the extent and intensity of voluntary association memberships; and (2) tertiary participation through the mass media and junkets into the city. In addition to examining the structure of social participation in a black community, it is a major purpose of this monograph to look at two types of variation in such patterns: variations due to income and to the effects of a short-range move into new housing within the Boston black community.

FOOTNOTES

(Chapter I)

[1]Louis Wirth, "Urbanism as a Way of Life," <u>American Journal of Sociology</u>, <u>44</u> (1938), 1-24.

[2]<u>Ibid</u>., pp. 20-21.

[3]Maurice R. Stein, <u>The Eclipse of Community</u> (New York: Harper Torchbook, 1964), pp. 283-284.

[4]<u>Ibid</u>., p. 331.

[5]Herbert Marcuse, <u>One-Dimensional Man</u> (Boston: Beacon Press, 1964), p. 246.

[6]Robert A. Nisbet, <u>Community and Power</u> (New York: Oxford University Press, 1962), p. xi.

[7]<u>Ibid</u>., p.53.

[8]<u>Vide</u> William Kornhauser, <u>The Politics of Mass Society</u> (Glencoe, Illinois: Free Press, 1959), pp. 143ff.; and Philip M. Hauser, "On the Impact of Urbanism on Social Organization, Human Nature and the Political Order," <u>Confluence</u>, <u>7</u> (1958), 57-69.

[9]Wendell Bell and Marion D. Boat, "Urban Neighhorhoods, and Informal Social Relations," <u>The American Journal of Sociology</u>, <u>62</u> (1957), 391-398; Murray Hausknecht, <u>The Joiners</u> (New York: Bedminster Press, 1962); and Scott Greer, <u>The Emerging City</u> (New York: The Free Press of Glencoe, 1962), pp. 90ff.

[10]Ernest W. Burgess, "Growth of the City: An Introduction to a Research Project," <u>Studies in Human Ecology</u>, ed. George A. Theodorson (New York: Harper and Row, 1961), pp. 37-44.

[11]C. R. Shaw, <u>Delinquency Areas</u> (Chicago: University of Chicago Press, 1929); and H. W. Zorbaugh, <u>The Gold Coast and the Slum</u> (Chicago: University of Chicago Press, 1929).

[12]Zorbaugh, <u>op. cit</u>., pp. 128ff.

[13]R. D. McKenzie, "The Neighborhood: A Study of Local Life in the City of Columbus, Ohio," <u>American Journal of Sociology</u>, <u>27</u> (1922), 506.

[14]C. C. North, <u>Social Differentiation</u> (Chaptel Hill, North Carolina: University of North Carolina Press, 1927), pp. 247f.

[15]Genevieve Knupfer, "Portrait of the Underdog," <u>Class, Status and Power</u>, ed. Reinhard Bendix and Seymour M. Lipset (Glencoe, Illinois: Free Press, 1953), p. 257.

[16] Herbert J. Gans, The Urban Villagers (New York: The Free Press of Glencoe, 1962), pp. 305ff.

[17] William F. Whyte, "Social Organization in the Slums," American Sociological Review, 8 (1943), 34-39.

[18] William F. Whyte, Street Corner Society (2d ed.; Chicago: University of Chicago Press, 1955).

[19] Gans, op. cit.

[20] Ibid., pp. 80-81.

[21] Vide, for example, Louis Wirth, The Ghetto (Chicago: University of Chicago Press, 1928).

[22] Gunnar Myrdal, An American Dilemma (New York: McGraw-Hill Paperback, 1964), II, 952-953.

[23] Kenneth B. Clark, Dark Ghetto (New York: Harper and Row, 1965), p. 81.

[24] Ibid., p. 174.

[25] Office of Policy Planning and Research, United States Department of Labor, The Negro Family: the Case for National Action (Washington: Government Printing Office, 1965), pp. 4-6, 47-48. Cf. also E. Franklin Frazier, The Negro Family in Chicago (Chicago: University of Chicago Press, 1932).

[26] Lee Rainwater, "Crucible of Identity: The Negro Lower-Class Family," Daedalus, 95 (1966), 205.

[27] Lewis G. Watts et al., The Middle-Income Negro Family Faces Urban Renewal (Commonwealth of Massachusetts, 1964), pp. 56-57, 90.

[28] The 1964 Report of Boston's Fair Housing, Inc., a service listing housing available on an "equal opportunity" basis, indicated that 107 listings had been sent in to them by local real estate brokers, Fair Housing Committees, and individual owners. Many of the outer suburbs and some of the intra-city districts were represented in the listings. At the same time, they had only 99 black families on their rolls actively seeking housing. Thus, the supply slightly exceeds the demand. Many of those who have been helped to find new housing voluntarily located in segregated areas. These facts at least suggest that discrimination in the housing market is not the only factor accounting for the non-migration of middle-class blacks. Lest it be said that non-migration is only a middle-class phenomenon, testimony of public housing officials, now under pressure to place blacks throughout the city, indicates that the 20% of public housing applicants who are black prefer black projects. Most of them turn down predominantly white projects, even to the point of remaining on a long waiting list for a segregated project. These latter data undoubtedly contain an element of rationalization and must be interpreted with caution; however, they do not contradict the data on middle-income families.

[29] "Leaders" were chosen arbitrarily from among those who often appear in the Roxbury City-News as officers of social, recreational, welfare,

religious, and political organizations. No claim is made for the randomness of the sample, only for the suggestiveness of their answers.

[30]Allison Davis, Burleigh B. Gardner, and Mary R. Gardner, Deep South (Chicago: University of Chicago Press, 1941).

[31]Hortense Powdermaker, After Freedom: A Cultural Study in the Deep South (New York: The Viking Press, 1939); and John Dollard, Caste and Class in a Southern Town (3rd ed.; Garden City: Doubleday Anchor Books, 1949). Cf. also Hylan Lewis, Blackways of Kent (New Haven: College and University Press Paperback, 1964); and Frank F. Lee, Negro and White in Connecticut Town (New Haven: College and University Press Paperback, 1961).

[32]Clark, op.cit.

[33]Nathan Glazer and Daniel Patrick Moynihan, Beyond the Melting Pot (Cambridge: The M. I. T. Press and Harvard University Press, 1963).

[34]St. Clair Drake and Horace R. Cayton, Black Metropolis (New York: Harper Torchbooks, 1962), Vol. II. Studies have also been done on Negro "power elites." Vide, for example, M. Elaine Burgess, Negro Leadership in a Southern City (New Haven: College and University Press Paperback, 1962).

[35]Nicholas Babchuk and Ralph V. Thompson, "The Voluntary Associations of Negroes," American Sociological Review, 27 (1962), 647-655.

[36]Kathryn P. Meadow, "Negro-White Differences Among Newcomers to a Transitional Urban Area," The Journal of Intergroup Relations, 3 (1962), 320-330.

[37]Daniel M. Wilner et al., The Housing Environment and Family Life (Baltimore: The Johns Hopkins Press, 1962); and Peter Marris, Family and Social Change in an African City (Chicago: Northwestern University Press, 1962).

[38]Werner S. Landecker, "Types of Integration and their Measurement," American Journal of Sociology, 56 (1951), 332-340.

[39]Elihu Katz and Paul F. Lazarsfeld, Personal Influence (New York: Free Press Paperback, 1964), p. 44. Their emphasis.

CHAPTER II

BOSTON: THE CITY AND THE SAMPLE

The City

    Boston is a remarkable city in that many ethnic communities have persisted
for a long time beyond the first surges of immigrant settlement. In the mid-
1960's South Boston is still distinctively Irish; East Boston, Italian; Matta-
pan, Jewish.   Just south of the preponderantly Yankee Back Bay section of Boston and southwest of the downtown district is the Roxbury-South End-North
Dorchester area, a section of the city now containing most of Boston's black
population. Beginning at the middle of the nineteenth century the South End was
settled by white upper-class families. In the 1860's the northern part began to
see an invasion of working class families, while the rest was rapidly becoming
middle class and upper-class families were beginning to leave. Some fifty years
later the black population began to filter into this area from their original
residences nearer the core of the city.[1] "Over the next few decades Negroes
led by those of their group of the higher income brackets moved first into
the suburbs of Roxbury below Dudley Station and slowly and deliberately, following the main traffic arteries, expanded into Upper Roxbury and Dorchester."[2]
Much of the housing in this area, being abandoned by the former Irish and
Jewish inhabitants, had begun to deteriorate. "The homes available to them
were either inadequate buildings or adequate buildings on inadequate land,
and even before Negroes arrived Roxbury had become a neighborhood of houses
divided to keep each family's rent bill small."[3] Black Americans came to
replace the Jewish population of the area, which in its turn had generally replaced the Irish.
    Toward the beginning of World War II a significant influx of blacks from
southern and border states into the Boston area began to swell the size of the
ghetto community. In 1940 the black population in Boston was about 24,000;
from 1940 to 1960 the black population increased nearly threefold. As of the
1960 census, blacks were about 3% of the Boston SMSA population.[4] However,
this percentage is by no means distributed equally over all of the SMSA census
tracts. About 81% of the metropolitan area's black residents live in the city
of Boston proper; and about 98% of this number live in concentrated tracts in
the Roxbury area of Boston.[5] Included in the "Roxbury area" designation are
those disproportionately minority census tracts of the South End (including
the Back Bay edge) and North Dorchester which border on Roxbury proper. In
these three districts approximately 61,000 of Boston's 63,000 black residents
reside.[6] The core census tracts in Roxbury are more than 90% black; those
surrounding the core are disproportionately black.[7]
    The Roxbury area ghetto reflects the effects of both historical and
contemporary discrimination on the part of whites. The current focal point

of controversy between the minority subcommunity and the white power structure is de facto school segregation.[8] On occasion the black ghetto is viewed in "slum as jungle" terms by whites both inside and outside this city power structure. If such a label refers to certain pressing social problems which characterize the lives of some of the minority poor, in general the area partially fits the label. It does have a disproportionate share of Boston's housing dilapidation, school deterioration, reported crime, Aid to Families with Dependent Children, and reported juvenile delinquency. For example, for the city as a whole, 49% of nonwhite dwelling units are in deteriorated or dilapidated condition (according to the 1960 Census of Housing), while 21% of all dwelling units in the city are in such condition. Although nonwhites make up one-tenth of the city's population, they occupy more than one-fifth of the substandard dwelling units. These very units are also overcrowded.[9] Moreover, according to a data sheet published by the Boston Northern Student Movement, a private association providing tutorial and educational programs for disadvantaged children and their parents, the tuberculosis rate and infant mortality rate for the Roxbury area are among the highest in the state, as are the rates of juvenile delinquency and crime. Too often, however, an impression of personal and social disorganization, of anomie and social isolation, has come to dominate the image of the area. It is quite probable, though often overlooked, that a majority of the black working-class population carry on reasonably normal social lives, relatively unaffected by crime, juvenile delinquency, and anomie, and in spite of some housing and school dilapidation.[10] Nor does social isolation characterize their lives -- such is the general argument of this monograph.

The Sample

This report utilizes interview data obtained when I participated in an evaluation study of a low-income housing demonstration program in the Roxbury area carried out by the Boston Housing Authority with the financial assistance of the Department of Housing and Urban Development. Under the demonstration program a number of large low-income families displaced by urban renewal were enabled to move into new nonprofit, middle-income housing financed under FHA Section 221(d)3, a section which provides mortgage insurance for financing at a below-market interest rate. The low-income tenants pay rents according to their incomes; the difference between the rent charged and the amount they can afford is covered by the low-income housing demonstration grant.

Originally a matched set design was chosen for the evaluation; each of the rent supplementation families was to be matched with a similar family in two alternative Roxbury area housing markets, private housing and public housing, and also with a middle-income family moving into 221(d)3 housing at the same time as the supplementation family. Private housing names were secured from the Boston Redevelopment Authority (BRA); rent supplementation and public housing names, from the Boston Housing Authority (BHA); middle-income names from the private developers. The three low-income samples, public, private, and 221(d)3, were each to be matched on race, age, income, family type and size; the middle-income sample was to be matched on the same variables except, of course, income. The original interviewing design was as follows: each wife (wife of head or female head) in the four samples was to have been interviewed three times: before moving, approximately six weeks after, and six months after.

Some serious technical problems did arise. Two major ones developed in regard to the matching design. Since our original rent supplementation sample was to be selected by the Boston Housing Authority according to the rules governing the demonstration program, we had no control over the selection of the sample, which was intentionally composed of relatively large low-income families. Because of this we had decided on the aforesaid matching design in order that our alternative housing samples would be comparable to our basic sample, at least in regard to the major independent variables on which we could obtain preliminary data. Thus, we needed to obtain preliminary matching information on public housing families from the BHA, on middle-income families from 221(d)3 developers, and on private housing families from the BRA as soon as possible before such families were to move; this was in order that we might have at least three weeks for matching and for getting a successful interview, with those inevitable callbacks, before the family was actually in the trauma of moving.

Establishing regular channels for securing this information from diverse, and occasionally competitive, agencies in enough time before the anticipated move became a major difficulty. By the time fairly regular procedures for securing these names had been set up a number of possible matches were lost. To prevent as many losses as possible it was necessary to do some anticipatory matching, that is, to select a family coming into the private or public housing market before we received notice of the exact characteristics of the supplementation family. This is just one of the methodological problems involved in doing research in conjunction with public agencies. Such agencies are generally not oriented toward research, and their processing procedures seldom allow for the extra time needed for research intervention (particularly in before/after longitudinal studies). An additional restriction on the number of possible matches was the initial character of the basic rent supplementation sample; the number of large low-income Negro families in the BRA, BHA, and private developer pools for matching with the basic sample was usually insufficient. This fact primarily accounts for the reduced size of the public housing, private housing, and middle-income samples (see Table 2:1).

The original interviewing design, a "before" interview and two "after" interviews, was too optimistic. Although most wives were successfully interviewed one to three months before the move, two serious problems developed in regard to the "after" interviews. The interviewing design, as well as the hiring of interviewers and coders, was originally based upon a time-schedule set out by the housing officials at the beginning of the study: rent supplementation and middle-income families would be moving in from August to October, 1964 and again from March to May, 1965; private movers and public housing movers would also be moving at that time. Unlike one previous longitudinal study, that of Wilner and his associates, we had no control over the move-in dates of any of our sample families.[11] Private developers set the move-in dates for middle income and rent supplementation families; similarly the public housing authority and the Boston Redevelopment Authority had control over the move-in dates of the public housing and private housing families. These agencies were generally unable to coordinate their operations (and the move-in dates). Of course, respondents themselves sometimes varied their own move-in dates from those set by the agnecies, occasionally disrupting the interviewing time-schedule. These factors combined to produce an overall move-in pattern of families moving at several different times. The original plan was also vitiated by tardy construction completion and delays in selection procedures. Most of the samples actually moved between August and November, 1964 and between June and October, 1965; but some were moving in a few of the months in between. Since the largest group of families moved in about four to five months late, well past the original period designated for interviewing and well into the original tabulation stage, the final follow-up interviews on these particular families usually took place from one to ten weeks after their moves. For this reason and because of the problem of scheduling "after" interviews at (many) staggered intervals, the idea of a short six weeks "after" interview was discarded at a relatively early date, and during the months of July to October, 1965 all families were given one long "after" interview, which included the extensive questions on social participation used in most of this analysis. An additional problem also developed: some of the families who had been predicted to move on the basis of preliminary information from agencies decided not to move. This resulted in the group of private non-movers now included in the general sample.

Such research problems are generated by the nature of intervention in real social processes, particularly those (an increasing number) under the sponsorship of public agencies. Longitudinal research on the effects of job retraining, of literacy programs, or of poverty programs would undoubtedly face similar methodological problems.

Since it is not the purpose of this report to provide a general discussion of the implications of these methodological problems for sociological research, the basic characteristics of the black samples actually interviewed before and after their moves can now be examined. For the purposes of this report the original matched set design will not be used. The reduced sample of rent supplementation families with completely matched sets is on the order of four or five. Since the selection of families for the alternative housing samples was aimed at matching them with large low-income rent supplementation families, I will be dealing mainly with roughly matched housing subsamples rather than with matched individuals when I examine the effects of a move on the social participation of these Negroes. The chapters on social participation will deal mainly with the collected sample of all four original housing samples, together with a fifth group consisting of non-movers who remained in private housing.[12] Altogether this collected sample includes 120 black wives. Table 2:1 indicates the numerical breakdown by the housing subsamples.

The representativeness of this black sample can be examined in two ways: (1) What proportion of large black families in these housing markets in August to November, 1964 and June to October, 1965 does the sample comprise? (2) How does the sample compare with what can be ascertained about the Boston Negro population from the 1960 census?

TABLE 2:1

BOSTON BLACK SAMPLES

	Number
Rent supplementation sample	35
Middle-income sample	29
Public housing sample	24
Private housing sample (movers)	16
Private housing sample (non-movers)	16
Total	120

16

The housing subsamples comprise, as measured by the available lists at the time of selection, the following approximate proportions of their corresponding housing markets: (1) 80% to 90% of those large black families moving into 221(d)3 housing in the Roxbury area; (2) 70% to 80% of those large low-income black families directly forced to find housing in the private market because of urban renewal; (3) 70% to 80% of those large black families seeking public housing accomodations. These estimates exclude families in the various markets during the months we were not interviewing between August, 1964 and October, 1965. At the specific time we entered the housing markets and for the population of large black families in those markets, our Roxbury area sample is more than just representative, including some 70% to 90% of the families in each of those markets at that time. Although reference will henceforth be made to the Roxbury area "sample," the group is in this sense a specialized (nearly total) population. One housing market is represented by only a few respondents in the sample of private movers: those moving into private housing in the Roxbury area during this time but not under the duress of urban renewal.

An argument can also be made for the representativeness of this sample vis-a-vis the Boston black population. The original matching design under the guidance of which these 120 respondents were chosen included four demographic variables: family type, age of wife, number of children, and income. It will be useful to examine the distribution of each of these variables for the Boston black population and to compare them with the Roxbury area sample's characteristics, as well as with the Boston white population.

Since the sample is composed of wives only, it is of interest to note the differences in age distribution between nonwhite and white females in the Boston area. About 40% of the nonwhite women in Boston are under twenty years of age, as compared with 30% of white women.[13] Approximately 47% of nonwhite females, compared to 43% of white females, fall into the "20 to 54" bracket. In the "over 54" bracket are 13% of nonwhite females and 27% of white females. These statistics are by way of introduction to Table 2:2. The figures there indicate the age distributions of the Boston nonwhite population and the Roxbury area sample. As can be seen, the housing sample was drawn predominantly from the younger age brackets, i.e., those women who are most likely to have large numbers of children still living at home.

TABLE 2:2

AGE DISTRIBUTION OF NONWHITE WOMEN

	Sample Adult Females (N=119)	Boston Adult Females[a] (N=20,938)
Between 20-34	61%	40%
Between 35-54	36	39
Over 54	3	21
Total	100%	100%

[a]U.S. Bureau of the Census, op. cit., p. 52

The housing subdivisions of the Boston Negro sample were generally matched for marital status. Table 2:3 indicates that the Boston nonwhite population has a greater percentage of women who are no longer married than the white population. This differentiation is accentuated by the data on the sample. Since all the respondents in the housing subsamples were selected so that they would be comparable to the rent supplementation respondents, and since these respondents were somewhat more likely to be in the no-longer-married category, the overall sample is composed of a larger percentage of "broken homes" than the general Boston white or nonwhite populations.

The housing subsamples were also matched on the number of children in the household. There are about 1.12 children per household head in the city of Boston as compared with 1.58 children per nonwhite household head.[14] The data on the black sample indicate a ratio of 4.5 children per household head, a figure dramatizing the large family character of the Boston sample.

TABLE 2:3

WOMEN OVER 14 NO LONGER MARRIED AND ONCE MARRIED

	Boston Black Sample		Boston Nonwhite[b] Population		Boston White[b] Population	
	Number[a]	Percent	Number	Percent	Number	Percent
Total now married	63	53%	11,987	63%	123,901	71%
Total separated, widowed, and divorced	56	47	6,849	37	51,685	29
Total	119	100%	18,836	100%	175,586	100%

[a]One respondent listed herself as "single"; no evidence of marriage was indicated elsewhere in the interview.

[b]U.S. Bureau of the Census, op. cit., p. 52.

The last variable on which the housing samples were matched was income. Sharp differences in income between the white and nonwhite populations are indicated in Table 2:4. Nonwhites make up about one-fifth of Boston families in the under $2,999 income bracket, although they are only 9% of the Boston population. Moveover, they comprise approximately one-twentieth of the families earning over $6,000. The Roxbury area sample's median income ($4,100) for the year 1965 is somewhat less than the 1959 figure for Boston nonwhites ($4,235), while the percentage of sample families with incomes under $3,999 is comparable to the percentage for the nonwhite population. However, the sample has a larger

18

percentage in the under $5,999 bracket than the city population of nonwhites and a smaller percentage under $2,999.

TABLE 2:4

FAMILY INCOME (YEARLY)

Income	Boston Negro Sample		Boston Nonwhite[b] Population		Boston White[b] Population	
	Number[a]	Percent	Number	Percent	Number	Percent
Under 2,999	24	21%	5,060	33%	22,299	15%
3,000-3,999	29	25	2,206	14	14,050	9
4,000-5,999	43	38	3,859	25	40,778	27
Over 6,000	18	16	4,341	28	71,622	48
Total	114	100%	15,466	100%	148,749	99%

[a]These figures are for the year 1964 and were taken from verified agency records. Six income figures were not obtainable.

[b]Calculated from U.S. Bureau of the Census, op. cit., pp. 14, 165. Figures are for the year 1959.

Of course, the relatively low-income character of the sample would be dramatized even more if it could be compared to 1964-1965 census data, currently not available. (The national median is up approximately 20% over the 1959 figure.) Chapter VII will analyze status variations within the sample. It should be noted at this point that the sample is composed, with a few exceptions, of working-class families. Thus, the nonwhite population of Boston is a younger one than the white population and has a greater number of female-headed families, and families with low incomes. It was from the black portion of this nonwhite population that the Roxbury area sample was drawn. As can be seen from the tables above, the collected sample is representative of the larger, younger, and poorer of these black families. The sample does not contain representatives of the unmarried portion of the black population, nor does it include respondents from the best paid portion of that minority population; it also contains 10% more female-headed families than the nonwhite population taken as a whole.

Research Procedures

The wives in our sample of black Bostonians were interviewed, in the cases of those who actually moved, before and after their move into a new housing environment.[15] Non-movers were interviewed twice, using the "before" and "after" schedules. All black respondents were interviewed by black interviewers. The "after the move" interview schedules, completed on all respondents between July 15 and October 15, 1965, contained the most extensive battery of items on social participation. Data on social participation presented in subsequent chapters are drawn from these schedules except for the before-after comparisons in Chapter VIII. A copy of this schedule may be secured by writing the author. Standard research procudures were followed in training interviewers and in coding the interview data; the error rate for coding was about .7% for fixed-response items and about 1.7% for openended questions. The tabulation of the data was accomplished with the aid of the Harvard Computation Laboratory.

FOOTNOTES

(Chapter II)

[1] Rheable M. Edwards, Laura B. Morris, and Robert M. Coard, "The Negro in Boston" (Action for Boston Community Development, 1961), p. 18. (Mimeographed.) Sam B. Warner, Jr., Streetcar Suburbs (Cambridge: Harvard University Press and The M. I. T. Press, 1962), pp. 68-97.

[2] Edwards, Morris, and Coard, op. cit., p. 10.

[3] Ibid., p. 11.

[4] U.S. Bureau of the Census, U.S. Censuses of Population and Housing: 1960. Census Tracts: Boston, Mass. Final Report PHC(1)-18. (Washington: Government Printing Office, 1962), p.14.

[5] Ibid.; and Edwards, Morris, and Coard, op. cit., p.48. In addition, 39% of the 14,616 Negroes living outside the city of Boston live in the half-century old Cambridge ghetto; another 31% live in predominantly Negro tracts of Lynn, Everett, Malden, Medford, and Newton.

[6] Edwards, Morris, and Coard, op. cit., p.48.

[7] U.S. Bureau of the Census, op. cit., pp. 14ff. and pp. 165ff. For additional data on the concentration of Negroes in a few census tracts vide Charles Tilly, "Metropolitan Boston's Social Structure," Social Structure and Human Problems in the Boston Metropolitan Area. Metropolitan Area Planning Council, Commonwealth of Massachusetts (Cambridge: Joint Center for Urban Studies, 1965), pp. 1-31.

[8] For a discussion of this important problem vide Massachusetts State Board of Education, Because It Is Right -- Educationally: Report of the Advisory Committee on Racial Imbalance and Education (Boston, 1965), especially pp. 27-28, 63, 87ff.

[9] U.S. Bureau of the Census, op. cit. Tabulated by districts in Edwards, Morris, and Coard, op. cit., pp. 49, 228ff. Negroes make up 92% of the Boston nonwhite population.

[10] This should not be construed as playing down the importance of removing the restrictive barriers of racial and economic oppression.

[11] Wilner et al., op. cit.

[12] Hereafter this collected sample will be referred to as the "Roxbury area sample." A few white families, also interviewed for the evaluation study, have been excluded from the following analysis, except where noted.

[13] U.S. Bureau of the Census, op. cit., p. 52. It should be noted that these 1960 census figures are based on data collected six years ago.

[14]Calculated from _ibid_., pp. 14, 165. The figures report "children under 18" per "head of a primary family."

[15]All of the 120 families resided in the Roxbury area when they were selected. By the "after" interview three of the private movers had moved to the fringe of the area (Jamaica Plain, South Dorchester), and two of the public housing families were placed in an East Boston project. They have been retained in the sample because their respective samples are rather small and because they maintain ties to the ghetto.

CHAPTER III

PRIMARY SOCIAL TIES

Social ties can be loosely grouped into three ranked categories: primary, secondary, and tertiary. Primary interaction, such as friendship, tends to involve more of an individual's whole personality than secondary or tertiary ties involve; that is, an individual's innermost self and desires are more likely to be known by his close friends than by his fellow PTA member or museum director. As noted earlier, Lazarsfeld and others have emphasized the importance of primary ties in the communication of basic social values and norms. In this sense, primary ties, such as friendship and kinship, are more important sources of communicative integration than secondary and tertiary ties. At the very least, primary ties filter communications received through other channels. This chapter will focus upon three basic types of primary relationships -- friendship, kinship, and neighboring. The two following chapters will examine secondary ties, that is, membership in voluntary associations, and teritiary ties, a variety of less intimate links into the urban social grid.

The general questions to which the subsequent data on primary social participation are addressed can be stated as follows: (1) What is the extent of intimate social interaction for black urbanites? (2) What is the intensity (frequency) of this interaction? (3) How does this extensiveness and intensity of participation compare with other relevant studies of white and black samples? and (4) To what degree is this intimate social interaction restricted to the black ghetto and its fringes? The analysis of theoretical issues and current research, presented in Chapter I, suggested these substantive questions. Each question will be examined in some detail in the specific discussions of the Boston data to follow. The conclusion to this chapter will summarize the general answers suggested by the Boston data.

Friendship

One important type of communicative integration into the urban social fabric is friendship, a social tie usually characterized by its high degree of intimacy. The friendship patterns of urban dwellers, slum dwellers and otherwise, have been investigated by several researchers. Two classic studies of friendship patterns can be mentioned. Over a decade ago Lazarsfeld and Merton did an analysis of friendship networks in two housing projects, one in New Jersey and one in Western Pennsylvania.[1] Respondents were asked to designate their three closest friends, whether they lived nearby or not. About 10% in both communities reported no close friends; the remaining 90% (some 1350 families) listed approximately 2,000 friends. Another study done in the

1930's by Lundberg and Lawsing found only three people completely isolated from friends in a New England Village of 256, using a sociometric type of data collection patterned after the method of J.L. Moreno.[2] In addition, several English and Australian researchers, particularly Mogey, Oeser, Hammond, Willmott, and Young, have completed research on friendship and kinship links in the urban (largely working-class) areas of the Commonwealth.[3] For example, in his Family and Neighborhood Mogey briefly examines fiendship patterns in the central city of Oxford.[4] He found that 60% of the families, interviewed there reported no friends, 30% reported one friend, and 10% reported more than one. However, only 30% of a group of comparable families who moved out to a new housing development ("housing estate") in the suburbs reported no friends. These figures suggest that, at least for the socioeconomic levels investigated, British urbanites tend to be more isolated from friends than Americans so far studied.

What do we know about the social and geographical extent of friendship in a black community? Very little, unfortunately. Babchuk and Thompson[5] have reported one quite condensed breakdown on the extensity of friendship but not its intensity.[6] Their data can be seen in column two of Table 3:1. The classic community studies, north and south, generally neglect the subject of friendship networks in black communities, although Deep South does discuss informal cliques.[7] Keeping a tally from newspaper records of social affairs, lists of church and association members, and field observation records, they counted twenty-six cliques in the black community of Natchez, Mississippi (5,000 persons). They were primarily interested in the "value homiphily" of friends, as Merton and Lazarsfeld call it; hence, their data tell us little about the extensiveness of friendship cliques in the Negro community.

Our study of black Bostonians in Roxbury and the surrounding area was designed to investigate in some detail both friendship intensity and extensity for individual blacks in a ghetto area.[8] Table 3:1 compares the distribution of the Roxbury sample with that of the black community in Lincoln, Nebraska. Since all previous studies, to my knowledge, have found at least a few isolates, the Lincoln sample is quite unusual. All of their respondents reported at least one "intimate friend"; in addition, a majority of the Lincoln respondents had four or more intimate friends. Such an extremely high degree of intimacy and friendship interlinkage was not found in the Boston ghetto. Four of the 120 respondents reported no friends; two-thirds of the rest reported three or fewer friendship links. They average three friends apiece. When compared with pessimistic prophecies of few primary contacts and high individualization for urbanites, the extent of friendship ties, foremost examples of primary links, is substantial. Of the 120 respondents 116 are tied into friendship networks, that is, are not isolated from at least this one major type of primary social contact.

TABLE 3:1

PERCENTAGE DISTRIBUTION OF FRIENDSHIPS

Number of Friends	Boston Black Sample[a] (N=120)	Lincoln Black Sample[b] (N=120)
0	3.3%	0.0%
1-3	68.4	45.0
4-5	20.8	35.0
6 or More	7.5	20.0
Total	100.0%	100.0%

[a]The Boston sample is composed os 120 female respondents.

[b]Adapted from Babchuk and Thompson, op. cit., p. 652. Their sample was composed of 60 males and 60 females.

Although she did not examine friendship extensity, Meadow did investigate the friendship sources for a Detroit sample of black families. Table 3:2 indicates her breakdown of friendship sources, compared with the Roxbury area sample sources.

TABLE 3:2

SOURCES OF FRIENDSHIPS

Sources	Boston Blacks	Detroit[a] Blacks
As neighbors	33.3%	35.1%
Through friend	6.4	16.2
Through organization	11.7	21.6
Grew up together (school)	16.5	8.1
At work	10.2	5.4
Through husband	3.8	10.8
Through children	3.5	n.d.
Through relative	3.2	n.d.
Other (vague references)	11.7	2.7
Total	100.3%	99.9%

[a]Adapted from Meadow, op.cit., p.329. Female household heads were the "preferred respondents." N.d. means "no data."

The percentage of respondents making friends because of physical proximity, i.e., as neighbors, is about the same for the Detroit and Boston Negro samples. The other percentages differ, with 10% more of the Detroit sample making friends "through a friend" and "through an organization." The black Bostonians reported a larger percentage of friendships made because the pair grew up together. They also reported 5% more friendships through their own work contacts and 7% less through the husband or his job. Since the Detroit sample was not coded for the possible source "through children," an important link into city life for many housewives, or for "through relatives," no comparison can be drawn in this respect. It is interesting to note that 3.5% of the friends reported by these urbanites had been made through their children and 3.2% through other relatives. The residual category is higher for the Roxbury housing study because vague codes, such as "at so-and-so's house," were classified here, rather than placed in friends or neighbors categories. If this were done, it might eliminate the 10% difference between the two samples on previous friends as sources.

Another important question concerning friendship interlinkage is: What is the intensity of contact with friends? In this country "social area" analysts have undertaken several detailed studies of frinedship interaction and its variation from one economic or familistic area to another. Greer and Kube selected four Los Angeles communities which were alike in relatively high social rank, but varied in degree of familism (a composite of the fertility ratio, women in the labor force, and number of single-family dwelling units).[9] They discovered that at least 70% of the female residents in each of the four areas visited with friends as often as once a month or more.[10] Bell and Boat completed a similar study in San Francisco; however, they allowed social rank to vary as well as familism. Axelrod conducted a comparable study in Detroit.[11] At least two-thirds of each of the Detroit and San Francisco samples, as with the previously mentioned Los Angeles samples, reportedly get together with friends once a month or more.[12] The level of isolation from friends (12.5%) for the high socioeconomic area in San Francisco corresponds with studies such as those of Merton and Lundberg. The San Francisco data also present a general impression of the extent of friendship in relatively low-income, large family areas, comparable to the Roxbury area of Boston. Even in the low socioeconomic area of San Francisco two-thirds of the subjects are in contact with friends once a month or more, although about one-fifth are quite isolated from friendship contacts. For black families, however, there is as yet little published data on friendship contact frequency. Thus Meadow reports tersely that 43% of her black respondents visited with friends at least three times a week.[13]

Each of the Roxbury area respondents was asked to list her friends until she ceased naming any. Each friend's detailed address was secured, together with the friendship source, the "getting together" contact frequency, and the phone contact frequency. One aside is worth inserting here. Any doubt as to whether respondents were listing friends or just "acquaintances" should be dispelled by the fact that all friends had to be listed by name and with a full and detailed address. Approximately 95% of these addresses were readily locatable on a Boston city map. Frequencies of "getting together" and phone contact were scored from 0 ("never see") to 6 ("three times a week or more often"). Then the intensity scores for the friends in each respondent's set were summed to get an overall friendship contact score. Table 3:3 gives the distribution of intensity scores for each of six proximity categories; each of the proximity categories is mutually exclusive, that is, "friends living within a 2000-foot radius" excludes those living within a 500-foot radius. Only 4.2% of the Roxbury respondents did not interact at all with friends.

TABLE 3:3

INTENSITY OF FRIENDSHIP CONTACTS CLASSIFIED
BY PROXIMITY: BOSTON SAMPLE (N=120)

	Intensity Score				
	None	5 or Less	6-15	16 or More	Total
Friends Living Within					
500' radius	70.8%	6.7	17.5	5.0	100.0%
2000' radius	75.0%	13.3	9.1	2.5	99.9%
1 mile radius	54.1%	16.7	23.3	6.0	100.1%
2 mile radius	65.8%	14.2	20.0	0.0	100.0%
In Boston SMSA	73.3%	15.0	10.9	.8	100.0%
Outside Boston SMSA	97.5%	1.6	.8	0.0	99.9%
Total Area (All Brackets)	4.2%	14.1	52.5	29.2	100.0%

About 82% had an intensity score of at least 6 (one friend seen three times a week or the equivalent), and 29% had a score greater than 16 (three friends seen twice a week or the equivalent). The mean contact score for the whole sample was a sizable 13.2, while the mean number of friends is three. Scanning the interview schedules reveals that such a score typically means that a given respondent has intensive contact (several times a week) with two friends and a tenuous ("seldom see") relationship with another. Although not directly comparable with the Detroit and San Francisco data, these figures suggest a level of friendship interaction at least as intensive as the earlier studies of whites and blacks, if not more intensive.[14] In any event, these Boston women are hardly isolated from intimate primary ties even in the midst of an ethnic slum area. They fit neither the stereotype of the isolated urban or the anonymous slum dweller; in fact, at least three quarters of them seem to be engaged in weekly (or nearly daily) friendship relations.

Several studies of neighboring have substantiated the contention that families neighbor with others most accessible to them.[15] This suggests the following hypothesis: urbanites tend to maintain friendships with persons who live close to them. Or, better, the overwhelming majority of friendships for a given group of urban residents will be drawn from the local residential community. Table 3:4 demonstrates this fact. For the whole distribution of 342 friendships one-third fall within a four-block radius (2000 feet) and two-thirds within a one-mile radius. As the distance from the respondents is roughly doubled (and the area is much more than doubled), the percentage of all friendships drawn from increasingly distant areas declines substantially, as does the mean number of friends for each successive category.

TABLE 3:4

NUMBER OF FRIENDS CLASSIFIED BY DISTANCE FROM RESPONDENT
BOSTON SAMPLE (N=120)

	Total Number of Friends	Percent	Cumulative Percent	Mean Number of Friends Per Respondent
Friends Living Within				
2000' radius	116	34.0%	34.0%	.97
1 mile radius	108	31.6	65.6	.90
2 mile radius	69	20.2	85.8	.58
In Boston SMSA	43	12.6	98.4	.36
Outside Boston SMSA	6	1.8	100.0	.05
Total	342	100.2%		

Since the area circumscribed by a circle with a radius of two miles and its center on a respondent would include virtually the entire Boston ghetto, and since some 86% of the friends of the Roxbury sample live within such a two-mile radius, the overwhelming majority of friends seem to live within the ghetto area. Plotting the addresses of all 342 friends listed by these black respondents definitely revealed that approximately 95% reside within the Roxbury-Dorchester-South End area.

Even within the ghetto, the areas nearer the respondent tend to provide the larger percentage of intimtate friends. The mean intensity of friendship contact also varies inversely with the distance, with the mean contact under one block equal to 5.64 and the contact for each increasingly larger area decreasing as one moves away from the respondent.

TABLE 3:5

MEAN INTENSITY CONTACT PER FRIEND
BOSTON SAMPLE (N=120)

	Mean Contact Per Friend
Friend Living Within	
500" radius	5.64
2000' radius	4.54
1 mile radius	4.41
2 mile radius	4.21
In Boston SMSA	4.16
Outside Boston SMSA	2.17

Summarizing these data, it is evident that these black urbanites draw their friends primarily from propinquant areas. The relationship between physical proximity and intensity of interaction also seems to be borne out; those friends who live farther away are less likely to be seen as often as those who live nearby.

Several of us who interviewed early in the Roxbury Study came to the conclusion that "getting together" is not the exclusive form of communicative contact between friends. Some of the first respondents commented to the effect that: "I don't see her much, but we talk every day on the phone." Thus, the follow-up interviews on which this chapter on primary ties is based included a listing of phone contact with all friends. The distribution of this contact can be seen in Table 3:6. Since intensity of phone communication was coded in exactly the same categories as visiting frequency, the mean amount of contact in each instance can be directly compared. The mean visitation score was 13.8, while the mean phone contact was somewhat less at 8.4 (6 is equivalent to one friend, called three-plus times a week), which is still high for these relatively low-income and low-middle-income "slum" families. Fewer low-income families have phones than others in the city. Phone installment rates are exorbitantly high in the Roxbury area; very large money deposits are required. In spite of this, the average black wife in our sample called some friend daily or at least several times a week.

TABLE 3:6

PHONE CONTACT WITH FRIENDS CLASSIFIED BY
DISTANCE OF FRIENDS FROM RESPONDENT
BOSTON BLACK SAMPLE (N=120)

	Percentage of Respondents			Mean Phone Contact Per Friend
	Never Phone	Phone	Total	
Friends Living Within				
500' radius	91.7%	8.3	100.0%	1.25
2000' radius	86.7%	13.3	100.0%	2.16
1 mile radius	66.7%	33.3	100.0%	3.51
2 mile radius	71.7%	28.3	100.0%	4.00
In Boston SMSA	83.3%	16.7	100.0%	2.98
Outside Boston SMSA	100.0%	0.0	100.0%	0.00

One hypothesis which suggested itself prior to the collection of this
telephone data was as follows: the farther friends live away from the
respondent, the more frequent will be the telephone interaction between them.
Early theorists of primary group interaction emphasized its face-to-face character,
but the telephone has become a communications link for primary group interaction, even though it does not involve face-to-face confrontation. The
significance of this communications link for respondents separated from their
friends by increasing distances can be seen in column five. The aforementioned hypothesis is supported by the data up to a point. Within the
two-mile radius friends living farther away have more phone contact with
the respondents, on the average, than friends living closer. For example,
the sixty-four friends living within 500 feet of the respondents had a
mean contact of 1.25, a figure representing a very low level of phone interaction for friends living within one block of each other. The figure for
interaction goes up by increments for friends living within each increasingly
distant cutoff point, at least up to two miles. This phenomenon may be due
to the fact that many in the sample have in the last few months moved from
one to two miles away from their previous residences; the fairly high (4.0)
average for the one-to-two-mile bracket may indicate continuing phone interaction
between friends now living at an inconvenient distance from one another. Phone
contact within the two-mile-to-SMSA radius is less intensive than in the one-
to-two-mile bracket, thus going against the direction of association suggested
by the hypothesis. However, even in this most distant bracket mean phone
contact per friend is higher than for the two brackets closest to the respondent.

The distribution of total contact with friends, including phone contact and visiting together, can be seen below.

TABLE 3:7

TOTAL CONTACT WITH FRIENDS: SUM OF PHONE CONTACT
AND "GETTING TOGETHER" FREQUENCY
BOSTON SAMPLE (N=120)

		Intensity Score			
None	1-5	6-10	11-15	16-24	25+
3.3%	7.5%	20.8%	11.7%	20%	36.7%

(Mean contact = 21.6)

A majority of the sample falls at a score of 16 or above, indicating substantial contact, in person and by phone, with friends in this particular black community. Approximately two-thirds of the sample have a contact intensity of 11 or greater. This is especially notable since a majority of the sample have lived in Boston less than fifteen years; in fact, three-quarters have come to Boston since World War II.

Summarizing, the general picture of black friendship ties seems to be quite normal, if "normal" means "similar to that presented by other studies of friendship." These housewives, either in spite of or perhaps because of their large numbers of children and low income, seem to have as many friends and as intensive friendship contacts as other urbanites, or for that matter, rural citizens. Certainly there are internal variations, as will be seen in a later chapter. On the whole, however, an average of nearly three friends and of daily to weekly contact with them does suggest that McKenzie was incorrect when he described the slum as an area where "individuals and family groups are living in enforced intimacy with people whom they naturally shun and avoid.[16]

Neighboring

About one-third of the Roxbury area sample's friendships came into being as a result of residential proximity; the respondent and her friends at some time lived in contiguous apartments or houses. The importance of such neighbors has long been recognized in the western world: the medieval Anglo-Saxon owed his loyalty to his "kith and kin," that is, his neighbors and his relatives. For several decades some rural and urban sociologists have contended that rural-urban migration has meant the disappearance of neighborhoods (in the rural meaning of the term).[17] They have said that the meaning of neighbor-hood is only residential for urbanites; neighbors are no more than nigh-dwellers. "Thus, if the city dweller speaks of somebody as his neighbor, he means that

the person referred to happens to live near him, perhaps within walking
distance, but he does not recognize any specific social obligations in
relation to this person."[18] Heberle goes on to argue that the "mutual aid"
type of neighboring characteristic of rural areas is virtually non-existent
in urban areas. This is an interesting hypothesis. Undoubtedly there is some
truth here: at least the content of "neighboring" may change from rural
to urban areas. Since urban neighboring is predicted to be on the decline
in general, one supporting this position would undoubtedly predict that
neighboring in a Negro slum is virtually extinct. Mutual aid should virtually
be unheard of. The Roxbury areas respondents were asked, "Do you think of this
area where you live as a neighborhood?" Three-quarters of them replied yes;
an additional 11% did not give an unequivocal "no." In addition, three-quarters
of all responses to a follow-up question on why they did (or did not) consider
the area a neighborhood indicated that they were thinking in terms of such
social considerations as mutual helpfulness, friendliness, and visiting
patterns. Prompted by Heberle's contention that the norm of mutual aid no
longer prevails in urban neighborhoods, I included a direct question on this
point: "Do you feel you owe it to a neighbor to help out when he or she is
sick?" Eighty-eight percent replied "yes" unconditionally; another 5% gave a
conditional "yes" answer. Admittedly, this question does not directly
measure behavior. But it does suggest what the norm is: the overwhelming
majority of these Negroes feel that they have a duty to aid their neighbors.
At the very least this does suggest that the rural-urban contrast drawn by
Heberle and others needs much further examination.

Commenting on the social phenomenon of neighboring, various journalists
and sociologists have spoken of it as an essentially middle-class phenomenon.
A strong argument in the literature runs something like this: other-directed
men in grey-flannel suits, Whyte's "organization men," live primarily in the
suburban areas bordering on our cities.[19] These men and their wives, persuaded
by the social ethic, intensively (and usually superficially) engage in clubbing
and neighboring. Some empirical support for this phenomenon has been adduced,
usually in the form of a case study of a suburb. Fava has, however, presented
evidence for more and less urban areas.[20] Using the Wallin neighboring scale,
she found that neighboring was distributed in gradient fashion, with the
outer suburbs having the highest average neighboring score. She argues that
the physical intimacy, low density, and homogeneity of the suburb favors
neighboring.

Shuval has argued that casual neighboring is affected by both class
position and ethnic origin, as have Knupfer and others.[21] The suggestion
has been that economic restraints, such as no facilities or monies for
entertaining, and the physical exhaustion of unskilled laborers, limit the
time and resources which a lower-class family has for social interaction.
In addition, several case studies, such as Middletown and Working-Class Suburb,
have found that working-class housewives have a certain suspiciousness of
others and are not very well socialized to the informal clubbing and neighboring.[22]

Using a sample of husbands and wives drawn from an Israeli housing
community, Shuval examined predisposition toward neighboring and found that
52% tended to enjoy it and 48% were at least a bit negative about it.
The percentage which was positively oriented went down with class position;
the lower-status respondents were the most negative. With regard to ethnicity
she found that "the Europeans indicate a lower predisposition to interpersonal

contact (45%) than do the non-Europeans (57%)," probably a cultural differential.[23] Europeans and non-Europeans likewise show a consistent decline in actual neighboring behavior as one moves down the status scale.

Several important studies which go more into detail on the extent of neighboring in the lower socioeconomic brackets should be noted. In an article cited previously, Bell and Boat reported the extent of neighboring for families in different areas of San Francisco. About 41% of the males in the high-familistic, low-economic-status area never visited with their neighbors; 31.5% of the males in the high-familistic, high-economic-status area did not get together with their neighbors at all.[24] The low-familistic areas had 50% or more respondents in the "never neighbor" bracket. For a sample of female respondents Greer and Kube found a similar phenomenon in Los Angeles. High-familistic areas had more neighboring than low-familistic ones.[25] One of the most important of these neighboring studies is that of Caplow, Stryker, and Wallace.[26] They investigated the extensiveness and intensity of neighboring in twenty-five barrios in San Juan, Puerto Rico, most of which were relatively low-income areas. One major difficulty in such research is the definition of a neighborhood. Some view neighborhoods as a physical unit such as a residential block; others conceptualize socially in terms of a network of interacting nigh-dwellers centered on an individual resident. In the San Juan study a neighborhood was arbitrarily defined as twenty physically contiguous dwellings. A family's knowledge of and interaction with the other nineteen families were the criteria for neighboring extensity and intensity. They found that only 3% of their 500 female household heads were completely isolated from their neighbors; that is, they did not know either their neighbors' names or their faces. The mean amount of neighboring on a scale running from 0 to 6 was 2.4, representing an average level of neighboring about the level of "stopping and talking regularly" with each neighbor ennumerated.[27]

The studies cited above give some idea of the greatly varying number of respondents (from 3% of females in San Juan to 41% of the males in one area of San Francisco) who are completely insulated from their neighbors; but the studies done in the continental United States suggest that the range is from 32% to 50% and that respondents with large families (in "high-familism" areas) consistently have higher levels of neighboring. However, these studies have generally dealt with white or mixed ethnic samples. Up to this point in time, only two studies have shed light on the extent of neighboring for black respondents alone. Meadow asked her Detroit sample "How many neighbors do you know well enough to call on?" The mean number of neighbors given by blacks was 2.58; fewer were named by those who had resided in the community less than nine months than by those who had been there longer than nine months.[28] This difference did not exist for the white families in the sample. Based on extensive interviews with black housewives, another study in a Baltimore slum revealed that 27% of them did no visiting with their neighbors.[29]

Table 3:8 indicates the questions asked of and answers given by the Roxbury area subjects. The questions are ordered from less (A.) to more (C.) intimate levels of neighboring; respondents tend to know more names than people and talk more often with neighbors than visit in their homes. As can be seen, 34% of these housewives have done no visiting of their neighbors -- at least in their neighbor's homes. Twenty-three percent have not talked with any of their neighbors and 21% do not know the names of any of their neighbors.

These data seem to jibe relatively well with those for the Baltimore sample just noted above. The data suggest that two-thirds of the Roxbury area respondents know at least one or two of their neighbors well enough to have visited in their homes; this may mean an average number of neighbors somewhat lower than that found by Meadow in her Detroit study.

TABLE 3:8

NEIGHBORING ITEMS
BOSTON SAMPLE (N=120)

Answers	Percentages		
	Question A[a]	Question B[b]	Question C[c]
None	20.8%	23.3%	34.2%
1-2	33.3	45.0	35.8
3-5	24.2	18.3	16.7
6 or more	20.0	13.3	12.5
No answer given	1.7	0.0	.8
Total	100.0%	99.9%	100.0%

[a]Question A: "How many of the names of your neighbors do you know?"

[b]Question B: "How many of your neighbors do you talk with often?"

[c]Question C: "How many of your neighbors' apartments (or houses) have you been in since you moved here?"

The items are clearly ordered, and their coded scores can be sumed to create a total neighboring scale. The figures in Table 3:9 indicate the overall distribution of scores on a scale which can range from 3 (no neighboring whatever) to 12 (extremely intensive neighboring).

TABLE 3:9

TOTAL NEIGHBORING SCORES
BOSTON SAMPLE (N=120)

Neighboring Score	Percentage
3 (None)/incomplete	14.2%
4-5	24.2
6-7	25.8
8-9	17.5
10-12	18.3
Total	100.0%

The mean score for the 120 black respondents was 6.6 Such an average score might mean for a typical respondent that she knows the names of, talks with, and has visited in the homes of two of her neighbors.

Approximately two-thirds of the entire Roxbury area sample have visited in their neighbors' homes, a neighboring figure which is all the more significant since it does not include visiting with neighbors in one's own home. Since the issue of status differences in neighboring is an important one in the literature, it is important to note that 63% of the low-income respondents in the Roxbury area sample have visited with their neighbors and that 75% of the middle-income respondents have so visited. But the order of magnitude of this visiting figure for the lower income respondents is roughly equivalent to that which Bell and Boat found for respondents in their high-familistic, high-economic-status neighborhood.[30] It is actually higher than that which they found for their low-income area. It is also about the same as the percentage (62%) which Greer and Kube found for their highest-familistic, high-income area in Los Angeles.[31] The overall 66% visiting figure for the combined Boston sample is not greatly different from the figure which Smith, Form and Stone found for their white midwestern sample.[32] These comparisons indicate that these black respondents are probably as well integrated with their neighbors as whites in various socioeconomic areas of our urban complexes. Most urbanites do have regular and relatively frequent contacts with some of their neighbors, and it would seem that the black families are no exception.

Kinship

A third type of primary social contact for urban residents is with relatives. Various classical sociologists, such as Simmel and Durkheim, have noted that the isolated (from extended kin) nuclear family is essential to geographical and social mobility in urban societies with a high degree of division of labor. More recent sociologists, such as Parsons, similarly argue that the independent and isolated nuclear family is a requisite for the development of an urban industrial society.[33] Tenuous ties with some extended kin may still exist, but they are of no major significance to the functioning of the nuclear family, since they no longer meet the prominent needs of the typical urban family.[34] This point of view suggests that urban families should seldom be involved with extended kin -- at least not regularly. And there should be a substantial difference between rural and urban kinship interaction. Until recently little empirical work had been done to substantiate or refute this point of view. Since the early 1950's, however, research has revealed that the extended family still exists in urban areas and performs a heterogeneous variety of services for the urban nuclear family, whether it be working-class or middle-class. Sussman and Burchinal have summarized the existing literature as follows:

(1) Disintegration of the extended family in urban areas because of lack of contact is unsupported and often the contrary situation is found.... (2) Extended family get-togethers and joint recreational activities with kin dominate the leisure time pursuits of urban working-class members. (3) Kinship visiting is a primary activity of urban dwelling and outranks visitation patterns found for friends, neighbors, and co-workers. (4) Among urban middle classes there is an

almost universal desire to have interaction with extended kin.... (5) The
family network extends between generational ties of conjugal units.
Some structures are identified as sibling bonds, "occasional kin groups,"
family circles and cousin clubs. These structures perform important
recreational, ceremonial, mutual aid, and often economic functions.[35]

The Bell and Boat study and the Axelrod study (previously cited) both point
up the continuing significance of these urban kinship ties. The differentiated
(by economic status) samples of Bell and Boat do not differ substantially
from Axelrod's general Detroit sample in extent of kinship interaction. From
42% to 49% of each of the three samples met with relatives weekly, if not more
frequently. From two-thirds to three-quarters saw relatives once a month or
more often. In a study of four differing Los Angeles samples Greer found
that from 49% to 55% of his female subjects had interpersonal contacts with
kin at least weekly; corresponding figures for once a month or more were
from 65% to 83%.[36] All of his samples were relatively high income; and
the areas with larger families and fewer working women had the larger amount
of kin contact. In a study in Wilmington, Delaware Charles Tilly found
comparable figures: 47% of his white-collar respondents and 54% of his
blue-collar respondents reported one or more visits per week with kin.[37] Thus,
the Detroit, Los Angeles, San Francisco and Wilmington studies have visiting
figures of roughly the same magnitude, with lower-status respondents tending
to have somewhat greater kin contact. More generally, Sussman and Slater
report findings on a random sample in the Cleveland SMSA; about 81% of their
families were found to be socially integrated with some kin in the Cleveland
area. No more than 25% of the families were isolated from kin with regard
to any dimension of interaction: telephone communications, visits, letters,
help received, or help given.[38]

Studies of blue-collar and working-class families have emphasized
the overwhelming importance of kin to such families. A graphic picture
of a kin-dominated society can be seen in Gans' The Urban Villagers, Kerr's
The People of Ship Street, Berger's Working-Class Suburb, or Dotson's New
Haven study.[39] For example, Dotson found that 30% of his working-class
families spent all of their spare time with kin; over half regularly visited
with some of their relatives.[40] Berger's extensive study of a working-class
suburban area revealed that kin contacts comprised the bulk of sociability
activities; about half of his sample visited with their kin "very often."
In fact, he quotes one blue-collar respondent who said: "I don't think it
pays to have a lot of friends -- maybe because we have so many relatives."[41]
Moreover, studies of urban areas in Europe have also found extensive kin
relations persisting among urban working classes.[42] Two studies of English
working-class families have indicated that 70% to 100% have regular or
occasional meetings with their kindred. Mogey found that regular kinship
contact was most extensive in the inner city of Oxford.[43] In a study of an
East London working-class borough researchers found very extensive participation in kin groups. For example, 31% of the men in their sample and 55%
of the women had seen their mother in the last twenty-four hours. Contact
with fathers and siblings was almost as extensive.[44]

But what of research on kinship ties of black families? Blumberg and
Bell report a study of 133 recent black migrants (females) to Philadelphia.[45]

About 88% of the respondents had relatives in the Philadelphia area; in fact, nearly two-thirds said they migrated there because of friends and relatives. Nearly half of these recent migrants reported that they visited with close relatives at least once a week, slighly less than two-thirds said they saw them at least once a month or more often. Relatives were very important in their move; 37% named relatives as first sources of information about housing.[46] Likewise Kiser found that relatives and friends were important sponsors of migration for blacks from St. Helena.[47] Tilly and Brown found that nearly half of their nonwhite respondents had migrated under the auspices of friends and relatives; approximately one-third mentioned relatives as very important reasons for their migration to Wilmington, Delaware.[48]

One Detroit study, previously noted, explicitly examined the extent of kinship contacts for urban Negro respondents. In Detroit 89% of the black sample had relatives living there, and about 65% of the total sample saw them weekly. Proximity was also found to be related to contact; "of the respondents with relatives living in Highland Park 85 percent of whites and Negroes see relatives at least once a week."[49]

Essentially similar to the Detroit findings, 84.2% of the Roxbury area sample has relatives in the Boston area (Table 3:10). Somewhat less than two-thirds had from one to three relatives in the area, while nearly a quarter had four or more here. While 16% of the Boston Negro sample had no relatives in the Boston area, 11% of the Detroit Negro sample and 12% of the Philadelphia Negro sample reported no relatives in their respective areas.[50] These figures show a remarkable similarity.

TABLE 3:10

PERCENTAGE DISTRIBUTION OF RELATIVES
BOSTON SAMPLE (N=120)

Number of Relatives in Boston	Percentage of Respondents
0	15.8%
1-3	61.7
4-5	8.3
6 or more	14.2
Total	100.0%

The mean number of relatives in the Boston area was 2.6 This is quite surprising in view of the fact that, of all urban ethnic families, blacks in northern areas tend to be recent arrivals. Approximately half of the sample have migrated to the Roxbury area since 1950; three-quarters have come since the beginning of World War II. If any families could be expected to be isolated from their kin, these predominantly southern and relatively recent migrants would be the ones. The data do not support this expectation; in fact, they seem to refute the contention that the typical black (nuclear) family is isolated from its kin.

The intensity of these kinship ties is of utmost importance. The weaker the bonds are, the more weighty the social change argument about "the weakening of the bonds of kinship."[51] Of course, a better way to examine change would be a before-and-after (inter-city) migration study of kinship contacts, but this has so far proved impracticable. Table 3:11 indicates the intensity of kinship contacts cross-tabulated by proximity for the Boston respondents. The coding for contact with each relative listed by the respondent was similar to that for friends, running from 0 ("never see") to 6 ("three times a week or more often"). The codes for each relative were summed to get total bracket scores (such as all kin within 500 feet) and to get an overall intensity score.

TABLE 3:11

PERCENTAGE OF BOSTON RESPONDENTS AT SEVERAL LEVELS OF
INTERACTION WITH KIN: BY DISTANCE OF KIN FROM RESPONDENT
(N=120)

	Intensity Score				
	None	5 or Less	6-15	16 or More	Total
Kin Living Within					
500' radius	90.8%	0.0	8.3	.8	99.9%
2000' radius	80.0%	9.2	10.0	.8	100.0%
1 mile radius	61.7%	10.8	22.5	5.0	100.0%
2 mile radius	58.3%	19.2	19.2	3.3	100.0%
In Boston SMSA	80.8%	10.0	6.7	2.5	100.0%
Outside Boston SMSA	0.0%	0.0	0.0	0.0	0.0%
Total Area (All Brackets)	18.3%	17.5	38.3	25.8	99.9%

The overall mean contact was 11.17; in the case of a typical respondent this usually means more than weekly contact with one relative and weekly or monthly contact with several other relatives.[52] About a quarter of the sample are involved in extensive kinship networks, a few with as many as ten relatives seen quite often. The bulk of the sample falls into the 6-15 intensity of interaction level, and about one-fifth are truly isolated from kin. Only one family actually had kin in the area with whom they did not interact at all.

It is rather difficult to compare these data in any detail with the findings of Blumberg and Bell or Meadow. The only way to compare these black Bostonians is to use the comparable intensity score for one weekly contact or more with one relative; this would be a score of 5 or 6. Since a 5 or 6 score could be gained by seeing two (or more) relatives less often than weekly, perhaps it would be best just to compare those who had a score of

6 or greater. The number of those with a 6 which means less than weekly contact with two or more relatives is likely to be offset by the number with a 5 score who should be counted as seeing kin weekly. In any event, 64% of the sample had an intensity score of 6 or greater. This figure is roughly the same percentage as Meadow found in Detroit. In both cases, nearly two-thirds saw relatives once a week or more often; about 19% of the Boston sample and 14% of the Detroit sample seldom, or never, met with their relatives.[53] The latter figures include those who have no relatives in either area.

Research by Meadow and Sussman, among others, indicates that the closer the relatives live, the more intensive the interaction; or, perhaps, the more intensive, the greater the propinquity.[54] In any event, the proximity correlation does seem to be borne out for the Boston sample. Table 3:12 indicates that the average intensity of contact is greatest for those relatives in the one-block bracket. Mean intensity declines somewhat beyond that point. The proximity phenomenon becomes a bit clearer when the number of relatives is percentaged cumulatively across the spatial categories.

TABLE 3:12

PROXIMITY AND NUMBER OF KIN
BOSTON BLACK SAMPLE (N=120)

	Number of Kin	Cumulative Percentage	Mean Intensity of Contact Per Relative
Kin Living Within			
500' radius	14	4.8%	6.0
2000' radius	37	17.5	4.9
1 mile radius	102	52.5	4.4
2 mile radius	90	83.3	4.2
In Boston SMSA	49	100.0	3.9
Outside Boston SMSA	0	100.0%	0.0

A majority of all kin living in Boston live within a one-mile radius of the respondent; only 17% of the relatives live beyond the two-mile limit. Plotting the addresses of the 292 relatives listed by these Roxbury area respondents revealed that only ten live outside the Roxbury-Dorchester-South End area; thus, about 97% of the kin of these Boston Negro families live within the ghetto and its immediate fringe.

It has been found that the giving and receiving of aid between relatives is very important. Important types of aid given and received have included baby-sitting, help during illness, financial aid, help with housework, and business advice. One Detroit study reported that 30% of their female respondents had given financial aid to a relative; 12% had received business advice.[55] The time period within which this aid was exchanged was left unspecified for this predominantly white sample.

TABLE 3:13

RELATIVES AND MUTUAL AID
BOSTON SAMPLE (N=120)

Number of Times	Question A[a]		Question B[b]	
	Number of Respondents	Percentage	Number of Respondents	Percentage
None	94	78.3%	91	75.8%
Once	6	5.0	9	7.5
Two or more times	20	16.7	20	16.7
Total	120	100.0%	120	100.0%

[a]Question A; "How many times in the last year have you given money to a relative who was in financial trouble?"

[b]Question B: "How many times in the last year have you gotten personal or business advice from a relative?"

The Roxbury area subjects were asked how many times they had given financial aid and received personal or business advice from a relative; "in the last year" was the time span specified. Twenty-two percent reported having given aid at least once to a relative in financial trouble; 24% reported having received personal or business advice. The figure for financial aid does not appear to be greatly different from that of Sharp and Axelrod. The lower percentage having given financial aid may be a function of the shorter time period specified for the Roxbury area sample; the difference on giving advice between the Boston sample and the Detroit sample may be due to the inclusion of personal advice in the question. In regard to these two rather specific -- by no means exhaustive -- types of interpersonal aid the Roxbury area sample seems to be almost as involved with their kin as the general Detroit sample. One additional piece of information also suggests that relatives are important in times of a minor crisis, such as a move: about 48% of the Roxbury area respondents received aid from their kin in moving into their present home or apartment.

That ethnic slum, or ghetto, dwellers are enmeshed in "peer group" sociability is the suggestion of Herbert Gans from his research in Boston's West End. By "peer group" he means a group based primarily on ties of kinship and composed of relatives of roughly the same age and life cycle.[56] Siblings and cousins of the basic married couple, together with their husbands and wives, are the central nucleus of the peer group. Godparents and friends are members, but participate less frequently. Gans' illuminating account of the peer group gives no indication of either the percentage of West End kin groups which were predominantly composed of "peer" relatives or the extent of participation in such groups by the Italian population.

A relevant tabulation drawn from the Roxbury area data on kinship can be seen in Table 3:14.

TABLE 3:14

"NONPEER" VERSUS "PEER" RELATIVES
BOSTON SAMPLE (N=120)

	Number Seen Once a Month	Percent	Number Seen Once a Week or More	Percent
Peer Relatives	163	64%	114	62%
Nonpeer Relatives	91	36	70	38
Total	254	100%	184	100%

These black respondents listed 254 relatives as being seen once a month or more; 184 were listed as being seen once a week or more. In each case nearly two-thirds of those relatives listed were "peer" relatives in Gans sense of the term, that is, of roughly the same age and generation as the respondent. In addition, individual tabulations indicated that a majority of the Boston respondents were involved in a kinship network composed of 60% or more peer relatives; over one-third of the respondents were involved in a group which was 75% to 100% "peer" group in character. These data on black (primarily working-class) respondents would seem to bear out Gans' contention that kin-centered peer group society is a reflection of working-class orientation rather than just an Italian value system.

Conclusion

Four important research questions, noted at the beginnning of this chapter, can now be re-examined: (1) What is the extent of intimate social interaction for black residents? (2) What is the intensity (frequency) of this interaction? (3) How does this extensiveness and intensity of participation compare with other relevant studies of white and black samples? and (4) To what degree is this intimtate social interaction restricted to the black ghetto and its fringes? These are very important empirical questions, since various theorists of the city and of its black subcommunities have spoken of both in terms of their anonymity, impersonality, and social disorganization. The data on the Boston sample, composed of relatively large, low- and middle-income black families, clearly argue against this contention. Whether one examines friendship, neighboring, or kinship patterns, it must be admitted that these urban respondents are generally not isolated from intimate social ties. They average about three friends apiece; and they typically see two of these three several times a week, if not daily. In fact, several have a very large number of friendship ties, a few with as many as ten or eleven friends. These data compare quite favorably with studies of whites. In addition to this friendship interaction, these same black respondents also maintain regular ties with, on the average, 2.6 relatives beyond their immediate family; they usually see these relatives rather frequently, one or two typically being visited at least weekly. Surprisingly enough, in light of what is often said about isolation from kin of contemporary urbanites, well over three-quarters of these black families do have relatives in the Boston area; and nearly half of them received aid from these relatives in moving into their current apartments. The data on kinship ties present a picture broadly similar to that of studies of working-class whites. Nor is neighboring nonexistent for these female respondents. Two-thirds of them have done some visiting in their neighbors' homes, and they appear to be even less isolated from their neighbors than whites in certain higher-income areas have been found to be. Three-quarters consider their area a neighborhood and tend to see it in personal terms, while nine-tenths of them believe it to be their duty to come to the aid of a nigh-dweller when he or she is incapacitated by illness.

The fourth question, "To what extent is this informal interaction restricted to the ghetto area and its fringes?", raises the basic issue of the effect of a ghetto area upon its inhabitants. In Boston's West End, Gans found that his Italian working-class respondents were intimately involved in informal social relationships, centered around kin-based peer group societies. But these were whites who are not as likely to be hemmed in by discrimination as black families. In addition to being working-class, the Roxbury area sample is Negro. Although Gans gives little indication of the existence of friendship and kinship ties beyond the West End, it is likely that they did exist to a greater extent than they do for Negro respondents, who are more severely hampered by their color. It is plausible, then, to see the black ghetto as intensifying those sociability characteristics of working-class life which Gans, and others, have discovered. This is borne out by two important statistics from the Roxbury area sample. Approximately 95% of the 350-plus friends of these black respondents reside within the Roxbury-Dorchester-South End area, an area with a core of extremely segregated census tracts surrounded by somewhat less segregated, but still concentrated, tracts. And approximately 97% of the 300-plus relatives of these Negro families also live within the general ghetto area.

Both of these figures strongly suggest the effect of segregation and concurrent proximity factors upon the social ties of black families. Their friendship and kinship ties are largely encapsulated; but ghetto restriction should not be construed to mean isolation, impersonality, or disorganization. Intimate personal ties are maintained even within the ethnic slum. The failure to see these positive aspects of ghetto social life, particularly friendship and kinship interlinkage, can seriously bias the attitudes of those who deal at a policy level with what is usually termed "slum disorganization." For example, in a Puerto Rican slum the activities of social workers, insensitive to slum social organization, actually increased the distress and social disorganization of the families involved.[58] Thus, policy based on the "slum as disorganization" pictures of Knupfer, Myrdal, or Clark can itself act as a self-fulfilling prophecy.

42

FOOTNOTES

(Chapter III)

[1]Paul F. Lazarsfeld and Robert K. Merton, "Friendship as Social Process: A Substantive and Methodological Analysis," _Sociological Research_, Vol. I; _A Case Approach_, Matilda White Riley (New York: Harcourt, Brace and World, Inc., 1963), pp. 513-530.

[2]George A. Lundberg and Margaret Lawsing, "The Sociograph of Some Community Relations," _Sociological Research_, Vol. I: _A Case Approach_, Matilda White Riley (New York: Harcourt, Brace and World, Inc., 1963), pp. 141-152.

[3]J. M. Mogey, _Family and Neighborhood_ (London: Oxford University Press, 1956); O.A. Oeser and S. B. Hammond (eds.) _Social Structure and Personality in a City_ (London: Routledge and Kegan Paul, Ltd., 1954); and Michael Young and Peter Willmott, _Family and Kinship in East London_ (Baltimore: Penguin Books, 1957).

[4]Mogey, _op. cit._, p. 96.

[5]Babchuk and Thompson, _op. cit._, p. 652.

[6]"Extensity" will hereafter be used to refer to the number of social ties of a given type, while "intensity" will be used as a term alluding to the significance (frequency, etc.) of such ties.

[7]Davis, Gardner, and Gardner, _op. cit._, pp. 208ff.

[8]The exact questions asked of respondents can be seen in the copy of the follow-up questionnaire available from the author.

[9]Scott Greer and Ella Kube, "Urbanism and Social Structure: A Los Angeles Study," _Community Structure and Analysis_, ed. Marvin B. Sussman (New York: Thomas Y. Crowell, 1959). pp. 93-112.

[10]_Ibid._, p. 103.

[11]Morris Axelrod, "Urban Structure and Social Participation," _Cities and Society_, eds. Paul K. Hatt and Albert J. Reiss, Jr. (New York: The Free Press of Glencoe, 1957), p. 726.

[12]It should be noted that the San Francisco data are from interviews with male respondents; the Los Angeles data, from interviews with female respondents; the Detroit data, presumably from both male and female respondents.

[13]Meadow, _op. cit._, p. 328.

[14]The mean intensity contact _per friend_ was 4.5, indicating an average level of friendship interaction midway between "three times a month" (coded 4) and "1-2 times a week" (coded 5).

[15]Leon Festinger, Stanley Schacter, and Kurt Back, Social Pressures in Informal Groups (New York: Harper and Row, 1950); Theodore Caplow and Robert Forman, "Neighborhood Interaction in a Homogeneous Community," American Sociological Review, 15 (1950), 357-366; and Joel Smith, William H. Form, and Gregory P. Stone, "Local Intimacy in a Middle-Sized City," American Journal of Sociology, 60 (1954), 276-284.

[16]McKenzie, op. cit., p. 506.

[17]Vide, for example, Rudolf Heberle, "The Normative Element in Neighborhood Relations," The Pacific Sociological Review, 3 (1960), 3-11; and Wirth, "Urbanism as a Way of Life," loc. cit.

[18]Ibid., p. 7.

[19]William H. Whyte, Jr., The Organization Man (Garden City: Doubleday Anchor Books, 1956), pp. 190ff.; and J.R. Seeley, R.A. Sim, and E.W. Loosley, Crestwood Heights (New York: Wiley Science Editions, 1963).

[20]Sylvia F. Fava, "Contrasts in Neighboring: New York City and a Suburban Community," The Suburban Community, ed. William M. Dobriner (New York: G.P. Putnam's Sons, 1958), pp. 126-129.

[21]Judith T. Shuval, "Class and Ethnic Correlates of Casual Neighboring," American Sociological Review, 21 (1956), pp. 453f.; and Knupfer, op. cit.

[22]Robert Lynd and Helen Lynd, Middletown (New York: Harcourt, Brace and Co., 1929); and Bennett M. Berger, Working-Class Suburb (Berkeley: University of California Press, 1960).

[23]Shuval, op. cit., p. 455.

[24]Bell and Boat, op. cit., p. 394

[25]Greer and Kube, op. cit., p. 103. Axelrod (op. cit.) reported that 50% of his general sample associated with neighbors less often than once monthly. Smith, Form, and Stone (op. cit.) reported that 30% of their midwestern sample never associated with their neighbors.

[26]Theodore Caplow, Sheldon Stryker, and Samuel E. Wallace, The Urban Ambience (New York: The Bedminster Press, 1964).

[27]Ibid., p. 155.

[28]Computed from a table in Meadow, op. cit., p. 325.

[29]Wilner et al., op. cit., p. 164.

[30]Supra, p. 55.

[31]Greer and Kube, op. cit., p. 103.

[32]Smith, Form, and Stone, op. cit., p. 278.

[33]Talcott Parsons and Robert Bales, _Family, Socialization and Interaction Process_ (Glencoe, Illinois: Free Press, 1955), pp. 3-33; and Talcott Parsons, _Essays in Sociological Theory_ (Rev. ed.; Glencoe, Illinois: Free Press, 1954), pp. 183ff.

[34]Wirth certainly plays down the significance of kinship ties in urban society. Wirth, "Urbanism as a Way of Life," _loc. cit_.

[35]Marvin B. Sussman and Lee Burchinal, "Kin Family Network: Unheralded Structure in Current Conceptualizations of Family Functioning," _Marriage and Family Living_, 24 (1962), pp. 236-237.

[36]Greer and Kube, _op. cit._, p. 103.

[37]Charles Tilly, _Migration to an American City_ (Wilmington, Delaware: Division of Urban Affairs, University of Delaware, 1965). Litwak found some-what fewer contacts in his sample from a study of Buffalo, New York. He reports that from 34% (upwardly mobile class) to 39% (stationary manual class) of his respondents reported receiving one or more family visits per week. Eugene Litwak, "Occupational Mobility and Extended Family Cohesion," _American Sociological Review_, 25 (1960), 15.

[38]Marvin B. Sussman and Sherwood B. Slater, "A Reappraisal of Urban Kin Networks: Empirical Evidence," Paper given at the 58th Annual Meeting of the American Sociological Association, Los Angeles, California, August 28, 1963.

[39]Gans, _op. cit._; Berger, _op. cit._; Madeline Kerr, _The People of Ship Street_ (London: Routledge and Kegan Paul, Ltd., 1958); and Floyd Dotson, "Patterns of Voluntary Associations Among Working-Class Families," _American Sociological Review_, 16 (1951), 687-693.

[40]Dotson, _op. cit._, p. 691.

[41]Berger, _op. cit._, p. 68. Cf. also A.K. Cohen and H.M. Hodges, "Characteristics of the Lower-Blue-Collar-Class," _Social Problems_, 10 (1963), 303-334.

[42]Kerr, _op. cit._; Mogey, _op. cit._; Young and Willmont, _op. cit._; and Richard Hoggart, _The Uses of Literacy_ (Boston: Beacon Paperback, 1961).

[43]Mogey, _op. cit._, p. 81.

[44]Young and Willmont, _op. cit._, pp. 46, 76ff.

[45]Leonard Blumberg and Robert R. Bell, "Urban Migration and Kinship Ties," _Social Problems_, 6 (1959), 328-333.

[46]_Ibid._, p. 330. Marris (_op. cit._) reports on the major significance of kin in an African city.

[47]Clyde V. Kiser, _Sea Island to City: A Study of St. Helena Islanders in Harlem and Other Urban Centers_ (New York: Columbia University Press, 1952).

[48]Charles Tilly and Harold C. Brown, "On Uprooting, Kinship, and the Auspices of Migration " (unpublished paper, Joint Center for Urban Studies of the Massachusetts Institute of Technology and Harvard University, Cambridge, Massachusetts, 1964), p. 22.

[49]Meadow, op. cit., p. 328.

[50]Supra, p. 65.

[51]Wirth, "Urbanism as a Way of Life," loc. cit., pp. 20-21.

[52]The mean intensity contact per relative was 4.3, indicating an average level of interaction between "three times a month" (coded 4) and "one to two times a week" (coded 5).

[53]Supra, p. 66.

[54]Meadow, op. cit.; and Sussman and Slater, op. cit.

[55]Harry Sharp and Morris Axelrod, "Mutual Aid Among Relatives in an Urban Population," Principles of Sociology, ed. R. Freedman et al. (Rev. ed.; New York: Holt, Rhinehart, and Winston, 1952), pp. 436-437.

[56]Gans, op. cit., p. 74.

[57]Ibid., pp. 229f.

[58]Helen Safa, "The Female-Based Household in Public Housing: A Case Study in Puerto Rico," Human Organization, 24 (1965), 135-139.

CHAPTER IV

VOLUNTARY ASSOCIATIONS

Ever since Alexis de Tocqueville reported on the importance of voluntary
associations in the United States in the 1830's, social historians and sociologists have devoted important time to studying the proliferation of such
associations. One of the significant issues with which sociologists interested
in secondary organizations have been concerned is the argument that secondary
ties, including voluntary associational ties, have replaced primary social relationships for the typical urban dweller.[1] As noted previously, Wirth's contention
that the urban social way of life is characterized by the "substitution of secondary for primary contacts" has been echoed by various writers on community life
and urban society.[2] Many such writers see contemporary urbanites as caught up
in a complex world of secondary ties, including participation in a plethora of
voluntary associations. However, national sample surveys have presented evidence
which seriously challenges this point of view, generally suggesting the direct
opposite: that a majority of contemporary urbanites do not maintain extensive
associational ties.

Hausknecht has reported in great detail the results of a 1955 NORC poll.
His figures indicate that the often cited extensiveness of associational membership in this country cannot, on the whole, be substantiated with survey data.
Only 36% of the national sample belonged to one or more voluntary associations,
including ancillary church organizations; only 16% belonged to two or more.
However, it should be noted that this poll excluded formal church memberships
and labor union memberships in its tabulations. An AIPO poll conducted a year
earlier turned up similar results.[3] The foregoing data are based upon a national
sample of respondents from all types of rural and urban areas. Hausknecht has
also analyzed the AIPO poll data by size of community. Contrary to what one
might predict from the Wirth position about the increasing extensiveness of
voluntary association membership as the character of an area becomes increasingly
urban, the AIPO data indicate that as the size and urbanism of a community
increase, the percentage of residents involved in associations actually decreases.
Of metropolitan dwellers 53% belong to no associations; but only 32% of small
town citizens are not so inclined.[4] At this point the relatively low degree of
urbanite contact with voluntary associations is evident; integration into the
social grid through this type of secondary contact does not exist for a majority
of metropolitan residents.

For our purposes here two further reclassifications of the poll data are
important: (1) What do the poll data indicate about the associational ties of
low-income metropolitan residents? (2) What do the poll data show about black
contacts with voluntary associations? Fortunately both classifications have been
made by Hausknecht.[5] Hausknecht's data indicate clearly that the pocket of

least interest in voluntary associations is to be found in the lower income sections of urban areas. Of metropolitan residents (those in cities with populations of 50,000 or more) making less than $3,000, some 63% of low-income persons do not belong to voluntary associations. The figure is 42% for smaller urban areas. Since ghetto areas, such as the Roxbury area, include a predominance of low-income families, one would predict from these poll data that associational links of Roxbury area residents would be less than for more affluent Americans, 50-70% of whom Hausknecht found involved in voluntary associations.

It is also instructive to examine national poll data by race and community size, as well as by income and community size. However, cross-classifications of this type have not been done. The only cross-tabulation which exists is a breakdown by race of respondent. Table 4:1 indicates the findings of a 1955 NORC survey of individual memberships.

TABLE 4:1

VOLUNTARY ASSOCIATION MEMBERSHIP
(NORC 1955)[a]

	Percent Belonging to		
	None	One or More	Total
For Individuals (NORC, 1955)			
Black	73%	27	100%
White	63%	37	100%

[a]Condensed and adapted from Hausknecht, op. cit., p. 62.

It can be seen from these national data that in the mid-1950's 10% more black individuals than whites belong to no associations at all. The percentage of black individuals who belong to no associations is very high (73%). Data from a comparable AIPO poll also indicate this same direction of difference, although the magnitude of the difference is less.[6] If the data were available for black respondents, one would also expect to find membership to vary with community size and income, effects noted previously for the general sample.

Several studies of black communities, such as Black Metropolis, Deep South, and Blackways of Kent, have touched on the question of voluntary association memberships of Negroes. In Deep South Davis and the Gardners virtually neglect social organization beyond classes and cliques, except for an occasional reference to the existence of fraternal clubs and churches.[7] No data are provided

on either the intensity or the extensiveness of these memberships. <u>Blackways</u>
<u>of Kent</u> is a study of a small black community in the South. There some general
observations on the extent of voluntary association are made: more than two-
thirds of the black adults had no organizational ties other than the church;
those really active in associations were even fewer. About 60%   held active
church memberships.[8]

    <u>Black Metropolis</u>, a study of Chicago's black community, allocates somewhat
more space to an impressionistic discussion of voluntary associations within
the black community. The predominant concern there is with the "black bourgeoisie," the rather small middle class:

> Middle-class individuals are great "joiners" and "belongers," and these
> organizations assume a special importance in a community where family
> background is not too important. They are organs by which aggressive
> individuals rise in the world and confirm their status.[9]

The authors discuss the proliferation of middle-class clubs and the extensiveness
of lower-class sect-churches in Chicago's Bronzeville, as well as upper-class
domination of the NAACP and the Urban League. However, the extent of associational
membership in the community is difficult to assess on the basis of their un-
focussed analysis. On the order of 30% of lower-class adults in Bronzeville seem
to be affiliated with churches. Otherwise, the lower class belongs to very few
formal organizations.[10] No estimate is made for the extent of middle-class participation in social clubs, but the impression is that the majority of middle-class
blacks are affiliated with such social clubs; no data are provided for other
types of associational ties.[11] The data for the upper class are even more hazy;
most of them seem to belong to upper-class clubs, fraternities, sororities, and
the NAACP.[12] On the whole, the organizational picture of the lowest-income
groups in Kent and Bronzeville does appear to agree with the poll data for
Negroes in the 1953 and 1955 national samples (NORC).

    Only two studies, to my knowledge, have attempted to systematically in-
vestigate voluntary association memberships for black Americans and provide
some statistical detail. One of these two studies was devoted to the questions
of (1) the extent to which blacks affiliate with formal voluntary associations
and (2) the variations in patterns of membership by social categories.[13] Using
a sample randomly chosen from the Negro ghetto, Babchuk and Thompson found that
three out of every four blacks interviewed were affiliated with at least one
voluntary association, even excluding church and union membership. Only 20% of
black skilled workers and 35% of unskilled workers were non-members, as compared
with the NORC poll's 73% figure for black respondents (excluding church and union
membership).[14] Babchuk and Thompson suggest that the striking differences
between their results and the NORC poll may be due to the inclusion of rural
respondents in the national sample. They conclude that their findings strongly
support Myrdal's point that Negroes belong to more voluntary associations than
whites.[15] A second study of associational memberships was done in the Highland
Park area of Detroit, Michigan. Again emphasizing black-white comparisons,
Meadow found that her small sample of predominantly female heads of household
distributed their memberships (including church and union memberships) as follows:
(1) no memberships, 31.6%; (2) one membership, 34.2%; (3) two memberships,
23.7%; and (4) three or more, 10.5%. She found that church or church-related
organization memberships accounted for 60% of the memberships of the blacks in
the Detroit sample.[16]

The questionnaires given to black respondents in Boston included questions on both wife's and husband's organizations. Babchuk and Thompson report number of memberships by sex, but they do not report on the intensity of the memberships or in any detail on the types of organizations; and Meadow does not report on sex differentiation or intensity, although she does report a breakdown on the types of organizational memberships.

Table 4:2 summarizes the findings of five studies which included black respondents. The two AIPO and NORC national samples include both urban and rural blacks, while the other three samples included only urban residents. It should be noted that the definition of "voluntary association membership" varies from sample to sample. Table 4:4 is arranged in order of inclusiveness, the studies with the least inclusive definitions at the bottom. The NORC poll and the Lincoln, Nebraska study did not include church or union affiliations as constituting memberships. The AIPO poll included union memberships but excluded church affiliation. The Detroit study and our Boston study included both church and union memberships as types of associational membership.

An additional complication in interpreting Table 4:2 is the varying sexual character of the samples. The national polls and the Lincoln study included males and females in the sample, while the Detroit sample included a few males. Only female respondents were interviewed in the Boston study. However, even with this complication four of the samples seem to have roughly the same order or magnitude of non-membership. The Boston and Detroit samples are the closest in character and in distribution of memberships, with 72% of the former and 68% of the latter maintaining associational ties. The AIPO poll has a somewhat larger figure for non-membership. The inclusion of church membership in its survey probably would have brought its non-membership percentage down around the level of that for the Boston and Detroit samples. Had the NORC poll included church and union membership, its large percentage of non-membership would also have been reduced, perhaps down to the same order as that for the AIPO, Boston and Detroit samples.

TABLE 4:2

VOLUNTARY ASSOCIATION MEMBERSHIPS OF BLACK INDIVIDUALS:
EVIDENCE FROM FIVE SAMPLES

	Percent Belonging to			
	None	One	Two or More	Total
NORC National Poll[a]	73%	18	9	100%
Lincoln, Nebraska Study[b]	25%	---75---		100%
AIPO National Poll[c]	46%	36	18	100%
Detroit, Michigan Study[d]	32%	34	34	100%
Boston Study[e]	28%	46	26	100%

[a]Hausknecht, op. cit., p. 62. Excludes church and union memberships.

[b]Babchuk and Thompson, op. cit., p. 650. Excludes church and union memberships.

[c]Hausknecht, op. cit., p. 62. Excludes church memberships.

[d]Meadow, op. cit., p. 326. Includes church and union memberships.

[e]Includes church and union memberships.

Taking these various factors into consideration, it appears that the same rough order of magnitude for non-membership characterizes these four samples. The one notable exception to this pattern is the Lincoln, Nebraska sample. The figure of 25% non-membership in the Table is the lowest for all five samples. Even this percentage is misleading, since it excludes church and union membership. According to Babchuk and Thompson only 12.5% of the Lincoln sample were not members of a church organization.[17] This finding does not jibe very well with any of the other findings on associational membership; it may be that the black community of Lincoln is unique in its organizational structure. It is, at the very least, substantially smaller (c. 3,000) than the Negro populations of Detroit and Boston (c. 60,000).[18]

The Lincoln study, however unique it may be, did examine sexual differences in associational membership. Males were more likely than females to belong to one or more associations.[19] In the Boston sample, by contrast, the males were somewhat less likely than females to have one or more associational memberships: males, 56.8%; females, 71.7%. However, the Boston data on male participation comes from the wife's report on her husband's organizations; wives may have underestimated the estent of their husbands' participation, perhaps through ignorance.

Most of the research on voluntary associations has dealt primarily with
the number or extensity of memberships. The crucial relationship of extensity
to intensity has only occasionally been measured even for whites; a few studies
of white samples give some clues to the intensity of organizational ties for
urbanites. For example, Scott found in his Vermont sample that the frequency
of attendance for each associational membership held was about one time per
month. Other measures of intensity indicated an associational "elite": the
holding of officerships and committeeships was the work of only a few in the
community; and 6% of the members paid about 49% of the total expenditures of their
organizations.[20] The Detroit Area Study also found that 24% of their associational members did not even attend meetings; and 72% had not given any time
to their organizations within the last three months.[21] The Boston study seems
to be the first research attempt to investigate _intensity_ of activity in
organizations for an adult sample of black respondents. As noted previously,
over two-thirds of these female respondents belonged to one or more organizations. However, the impact of organizational participation upon opinions,
norms, and behavior of the individual probably varies directly with the amount
of time which he or she spends in the organization. In coding the Boston
study data each organization listed by the respondent was scored one point for
membership, two points for attendance, three points for monetary contribution,
and four points for holding some associational office.[22] Thus the maximum intensity
score for any one organization would be ten.

Perhaps a comparison with a study using a similar measure of participation is in order. A recent study of Wilmington, Delaware gives a rough
idea of the average intensity of organizational contact for an urban sample
which included whites and nonwhites; the median participation score was 10.9
for the whole Wilmington sample, 6.5 for the blue-collar respondents and
21.4 for white-collar respondents.[23] For the predominantly blue-collar
Boston sample the mean organizational participation score for individual female
respondents was 6.4, and for families (including husband's intensity scores)
it was 9.1. Thus, the magnitude of these participation scores is roughly
similar to that which Tilly found for his sample of blue-collar workers in
Wilmington, only 50% of whom were black. An intensity level of 6.4 typically
would mean that the respondent was a member of one organization, attended its
meetings fairly regularly, and regularly made some monetary contribution to
it. Generally she would not be an officer in that organization. The mean extensity score for the sample of black Bostonians was 1.09 organizations per
respondent; an "average" female respondent in the Roxbury area sample would
belong to only one organization. The type of organization which receives the
greater proportion of participation time is religious; activity in the church
and its ancillary organizations consumes the overwhelming proportion of time
these Roxbury blacks have available for formal associations. This can be seen
in Table 4:3, which indicates the types of organizations in which the Boston
sample were active.

TABLE 4:3

TYPES OF VOLUNTARY ASSOCIATION MEMBERSHIPS
BOSTON SAMPLE (N=120)

Type of Organization	Mean Intensity Score	Mean Extensity Score
Religious	4.0	0.68
Civic	1.1	0.21
Business, Union Professional	0.3	0.06
Social, Recreational	0.9	0.13

The mean number of membership in church and related organizations is .68 member-ships; the means for civic, business and social organizations are much smaller, indicating their lesser significance in the social lives of these black re-spondents. This point is further substantiated by data from another question which asked for the extent of their contact with certain specified associa-tional settings within the local community. Of the 120 respondents 94% reported that they had not gone to a local tavern in the last two months; and 97% of them had not visited an important local "jazz joint" in the last two months. In reply to a question concerning participation in civil rights meetings, 84% reported no participation at all. These percentages, indicating a high degree of non-participation in certain types of secondary settings, corroborate the data on participation in civic, business and social organi-zations.

The previously mentioned Detroit study also examined types of organi-zations for blacks urbanites. Using the Boston study categories, 60.5% of Detroit memberships were religious, 16.2% were civic, 0% were business, and 21% were "social."[24] The Roxbury area sample was broadly similar, with 63.2% religious, 19.3% civic, 5.4% business, and 12.3% "social" affiliations.[25] Significant differences between the two appear in the business and social categories, the Boston blacks having somewhat more business memberships and somewhat fewer "social" affiliations. "Business" memberships include a few Boston wives who are members of a union.

These findings on the types of organizations to which blacks in Detroit and Boston belong suggest that one contention made by Babchuk and Thompson in regard to associational memberships may be in error. On the basis of their Nebraska data they have argued, following Myrdal, that blacks are more active in associations, particularly "expressive" associations, than whites because they are restricted from participation in the rest of society.[26] The data on associational ties in the Detroit and Boston studies give partial support to this point. The Detroit sample figure for one-plus associational memberships (including church and union) for blacks was 68%, and for whites, 59%.[27] The Boston figures were similar: 72% for blacks, and for eighteen comparable whites interviewed in connection with the housing study, 56%.

It does seem for these three studies that blacks tend to belong to associations somewhat more often than do whites. But Babchuk and Thompson, as well as Myrdal, also contend that blacks are involved, beyond the church, almost exclusively in expressive organizations, such as social-set clubs and recreational assoc- iations. Neither Babchuk nor Myrdal gives more than impressionistic data to support this position.[28] The Boston data suggest that a majority of associational ties are not to expressive organizations. In addition to church memberships there were 48 other associational memberships listed by members of the Roxbury housing sample. About two-thirds of these member- ships were in instrumental associations, such as the PTA, Marksdale Tenants' Association, and the Boardman parents' group, while one-third (excluding church ties) were in associations which were primarily expressive, such as social clubs and recreational leagues. Thus, memberships were two-to-one in favor of instrumental associations. In addition, a reading of about fifty weeks' issues (August, 1964 to August, 1965) of the Roxbury City-News, now called the Boston City-News, revealed the following breakdown of voluntary associations in the Roxbury area: (1) 30 churches and 4 church-related organizations; (2) 45 civic and welfare organizations, including 11 civil rights organizations; (3) 20 "social" and recreational organizations, including 6 fraternities and sororities; and (4) 2 union or business organizations. Altogether approximately 100 voluntary associations were mentioned, most only two or three times over the whole year, although a few civil rights organizations such as the NAACP and CORE were mentioned quite often. About one- third of these associations were churches; 45% were welfare or civic organi- zations, such as the South End Federation of Citizens' Organizations, or civil rights organizations. Only 20% had a strictly "social" or recreational cast. Again "instrumental" associations significantly outnumbered "expressive" associations, if church memberships are excluded.

The argument in reference to membership in a church is more difficult to assess. Presumably church organizations are both instrumental and expres- sive; the main-line Protestant and Catholic churches are certainly interested in changing the outside world, as well as their own members. In addition, they provide an opportunity for their members to express their religious emotions and gratify their own interests. Babchuk and Thompson assert that rank-and-file blacks are more active in churches than whites; this they suggest is due to the restrictive social environment.[29] That black Americans are more active is borne out by the studies cited above. In addition, they and others have argued that church attachments are made largely for expressive reasons; often the extreme emotional self-expression indulged in by certain sect members is taken to be characteristic of the religious life of black Americans.[30] However, the types of churches to which these urbanites belong have not been systematically investigated. Impressionistic accounts have been written concerning the proliferation of sects within minority communities, but little systematic data are available on the extent of participation on a community- wide basis. Only 35% of church members in the Boston sample belong to the more expressive sects, while 50% belong to the more traditional Catholic and and Protestant churches. The sect members comprise a substantial proportion of all church members, but they are not a majority, even of this predominantly low-income sample. Be that as it may, the question of the function of any church membership, whether in a sect or an orthodox church, for black Americans is still open. Church services may or may not serve a more expressive or

cathartic function for blacks than they do for comparable whites. This remains
to be investigated.

Conclusion

The discussion in this chapter has come to grips with one very important
secondary link into the urban social life: voluntary association membership.
Such membership, or the lack of it, has been a point of controversy, both
for students of urban life in general and for students of black communities.
The general problem can be stated as follows: Is the typical urbanite caught
up in a complex world of associational ties? The general evidence indicates
that a majority of urbanites are not members of voluntary associations, with
the possible exception of a church. Associations may abound in the city, but
their members are usually a minority of a given urban population. In addition
to the general issue, other researchers, such as Babchuk and Myrdal, have
argued that black Americans are the greatest "joiners" of all urbanites.

The Boston data do offer some support for the argument that black
urbanites belong to somewhat more associations than white urbanites; but the
differential is not striking, nor is it in the few other studies of black
and white urbanites. Otherwise the overall picture of associational activity
for these black respondents is comparable with the one conveyed by Komarovsky's
and Hausknecht's data on urban whites -- general non-participation. Excluding
church membership, a majority do not belong to voluntary associations. In
fact 28% belong to no associations whatever; and the memberships of the
remaining 72% are predominantly church affiliations, a fact supporting the general argument about the significance of the church for black respondents. Except for the church, voluntary associations seem to play a much less important
role in the lives of a majority of the black respondents than the primary social
ties discussed in the previous chapter; this points up the greater communicative significance of those primary ties.

Myrdal and Babchuk, among others, have also argued that the characteristic
type of association to which black joiners belong is "expressive," a term
almost equivalent to "pathological" in their discussions. Some impressionistic
data have been presented in support of this argument, but the significance
of expressive organizations in the overall associational life of the whole
black community is still a moot question. At least for the Boston sample,
representative as it is of relatively large families in the low- and low-
middle income brackets, data on non-church affiliations indicate a two-to-one
ratio in favor of memberships which are primarily instrumental. In contrast
to the arguments of Myrdal and Babchuk, it appears more probable that the
characteristic associational membership in a black community, bracketing the
question of church membership, is primarily instrumental. The argument in
regard to expressive significance of church memberships is more difficult to
assess. Admittedly, a majority of the church members in the Boston sample
do not belong to the extremely expressive sects but to main-line Protestant
and Catholic churches. This fact at least points up the need to reexamine
the usual image of black American religious life in urban areas.

An additional issue, also raised in the preceding chapter, relates to
the degree of encapsulation of the social ties of blacks within a ghetto
community. Plotting the addresses of those organizations listed by the
respondents insofar as their preciseness allows it to be done indicates that
almost all associational memberships are limited to the Roxbury-Dorchester-
South End area. Although the data on this point are not complete, they do

convey the image of black housewives limiting their associational memberships to the ghetto area. None are members of city-wide Democratic political committees or civic associations. Their associational ties appear to be encapsulated and outside city-wide centers of decision-making. Additional, and usually more tenuous, contacts with secondary organizations, including more impersonal settings than the typical voluntary association meeting, will be examined in the next chapter; the data there corroborate this phenomenon of the general restriction of activities to the black community. There is a great need for further research on the extensiveness of Negro associational ties and particularly on the significance which these ties have in the lives of black respondents and in the associational life of the city as a whole.

FOOTNOTES

(Chapter IV)

[1]It should be noted that voluntary associational membership represents only one important type of secondary contact. A list of other types would include participation in a work setting, participation in government, contact with social agencies, and contact with such organizations as libraries and museums. Nevertheless, voluntary association ties do seem to be one of the most important types of secondary contact for female respondents in that such contact often provides an environment for the making (and sustaining) of strong inter-personal ties; in this sense associations can occasionally be a bridge to primary social ties. (Vide Bell and Boat, op. cit.) An additional justi-fication for focussing upon this type of secondary tie is the growing body of literature available for comparative purposes. Chapter V will examine certain other types of secondary contact for which data are available.

[2]Wirth, "Urbanism as a Way of Life," loc. cit., pp.20-21; Stein, op. cit.,; Nisbet, op. cit.; and Marcuse, op. cit.

[3]Hausknecht, op. cit., p. 23.

[4]Ibid., p. 26. Komarovsky's data for New York City are similar. Vide Mirra Komarovsky, "The Voluntary Associations of Urban Dwellers," American Sociological Review, 11 (1946), 686-698.

[5]Hausknecht, op. cit.

[6]Ibid., p. 62.

[7]Davis, Gardner, and Gardner, op. cit., pp. 249ff.

[8]Lewis, op. cit., pp. 285ff.

[9]Drake and Cayton, op. cit., II, 669.

[10]Ibid., pp. 612ff.

[11]Ibid., pp. 688ff.

[12]Ibid., pp. 533ff.

[13]Babchuk and Thompson, op. cit.

[14]Ibid., p. 650.

[15]Ibid., pp. 652ff.

[16]Meadow, op. cit., p. 326.

[17]Babchuk and Thompson, op. cit., p. 651.

[18] Ibid., p. 649.

[19] Ibid., p. 652.

[20] John Scott, Jr., "Membership and Participation in Voluntary Associations," American Sociological Review, 22 (1957), 324f.

[21] Detroit Area Study, A Social Profile of Detroit (Ann Arbor: University of Michigan Press, 1952), cited in Babchuk and Thompson, op. cit., p. 649.

[22] The organizational scale used in the follow-up interviews is a revised version of Chapin's original social participation scale. F. Stuart Chapin, "Social Participation and Social Intelligence," American Sociological Review, 4 (1939), 157-168.

[23] Tilly, Migration to a American City, loc. cit., p. 33. Tilly's scoring of this scale allowed a few extra points for committee members who were also officers; otherwise the scoring was the same. This method of scoring would give higher scores for only a few Boston respondents and consequently would not significantly affect the mean.

[24] Meadow, op. cit., p. 327.

[25] The figure for church membership, as well as for non-participation, which Rubin reports for a mixed (white-Negro) Roxbury sample appears to be roughly equivalent to ours. Morton Rubin, "Negro Migration and Adjustment in Boston" (unpublished manuscript, Northeastern University, 1963), pp. 4-3 and 4-5.

[26] Babchuk and Thompson, op. cit., pp. 652ff. The term "instrumental" is defined by Babchuk to refer to groups which are formed to achieve "a change in some segment of society"; "expressive" groups are organized to "express or satisfy the interests of their members."

[27] Meadow, op. cit., p.326.

[28] Babchuk and Thompson, op. cit., pp. 652ff; and Myrdal, op. cit., II, 953ff.

[29] Ibid., pp. 654f.

[30] Cf. Clark, op. cit., pp. 174f; to a certain extent Myrdal (loc. cit.) shares this position.

CHAPTER V

TERTIARY PARTICIPATION

The social contacts of urbanites range from intimately personal ties
with friends and relatives, through voluntary association links, to a variety
of less intimate contacts with other people in relatively ephemeral and
impersonal situations. "Tertiary participation" will hereafter be used to
refer to two basic types of urban participation involving such tenuous social
contacts: (1) commercial trips and recreational ventures, including such
things as shopping and visiting museums;[1] and (2) para-social contact with
the mass media. The term "tertiary," admittedly covering a potpourri of
social contacts, is used here primarily as an organizing device, although it
does have some theoretical justification. Stein and other contemporary neo-
Wirthians have been preoccupied with an image of the impersonal city.[2] As
they have viewed it, impersonal and ephemeral social contacts are the lot of
the typical urban resident; for them such contacts are of central, not tertiary significance.
    However, recent rejections of the Wirthian view, citing extensive research
evidence, have pointed up the predominant significance of intimate personal
relationships for urban dwellers.[3] These social contacts involve strong bonds
of mutual interdependence and mutual obligations, such as the sharing of aid
and advice. Voluntary associational ties tend to be of secondary importance
to these same urbanites, although they too provide the milieu in which mutual
obligations develop between individuals and persist over time. The suggestion
here is that tertiary ties are, as their name suggests, of third importance
in the social lives of urbanites. They usually provide weak and ephemeral contacts between individuals; they seldom allow individuals to develop continuing
strong mutual obligations to one another as individuals. One example of the
lesser significance of these ties would be the ephemeral reaction of an individual to a message of approval (or disapproval) from someone in these impersonal
situations, such as a museum visitor or TV personality, as compared with his
more profound reaction to a similar message from a close friend or relative.
Certainly some communication occurs in these tertiary situations; and the
active individual does at least become familiar with the sights and geography
of his community and city. This being the case, such activity can be seen
as an additional bond tying the urbanite into the broader urban social fabric.
A survey of these contacts for the Boston sample is in order, both to indicate
their degree of contact with less personal social situations and to give a
fuller overall picture of their integration into the urban social fabric.
    One way that the individual urbanite is integrated into this social
fabric is through his or her regular ventures into the larger city area.
These ventures and activities undoubtedly have some information-gathering
and status-conferral function. They may also be very important alternative

sources of interpersonal contact, however tenuous, for those few who are completely isolated from primary contacts and voluntary associations. Certainly a strong argument for this point of view has been made in regard to the mass media; but it is also possible that trips into the city may have a similar function for those otherwise socially insulated.

Foley has suggested that the classical view of urban dwellers included an implication that urban residents make little use of local facilities. Urbanites were seen as "less locally self-sufficient in their use of facilities."[4] This was usually coupled with the idea that city dwellers went beyond the local area for facilities, such as stores, doctors' offices, and recreation, particularly since they become so very interdependent and unable to be self-supporting. Foley's data, taken from interviews with both sexes, indicated that the use of local facilities in St. Louis was quite substantial for most types of activities, but that different types of activities varied in the degree of encapsulation within the immediate locality. For example, 96% of food shopping was done in the local vicinity, although only 38% of doctor visits and 25% of shopping for clothes and furniture was done within the local vicinity.[5] The median distance for facility use was 1.2 miles, and 47% of facility uses were within one mile of the respondent's home.[6] Riemer and McNamara found that this figure was somewhat larger for housewives in Los Angeles; the mean distance for all social and commercial contacts there was 2.8 miles.[7]

The significance of the local community might conceivably be more important for black residents. In addition to the pull of the locality on the average urbanite, a force discovered in the studies reported by Foley and others, the strong primary ties of the black Bostonians, on the positive side, and subtle discrimination by whites, on the negative side, might encourage these black families to confine their commercial and recreational ventures to the local community area. The Roxbury area study went beyond the few other studies on locality use to include a number of questions on local and city-wide ventures beyond the household.

Table 5:1 reflects the distribution of responses on a battery of questions about recreational ventures into the broader urban area beyond the local black community. These women were asked how many times in the last two months they had done certain activities. With two exceptions at least eight out of ten replied that they had not done the mentioned activity.

TABLE 5:1

VENTURES INTO THE CITY
BOSTON SAMPLE (N=120)

	Not at All	N	Once or More	N	Total Percentage
Broader Urban Participation					
Gone downtown to movie	67%	(80)	33	(40)	100%
Gone downtown to public library	88%	(106)	12	(14)	100%
Gone to Fine Arts museum	91%	(109)	10	(11)	101%
Gone to Museum of Science	91%	(109)	10	(11)	101%
Gone to racetrack	93%	(112)	7	(8)	100%
Very Limited Contact					
Gone riding around in car for pleasure	42%	(50)	58	(70)	100%

Whether it was a trip to the racetrack or a trip to the Fine Arts Museum, the overwhelming majority had not made such a venture at all. Two of the more important activities for them include going downtown to the movies and riding around in the car for pleasure. Generally these activities involve the least interpersonal contact of all, at least beyond the kin and friends who occasionally accompany respondents in these activities. Undoubtedly the 8% who had gone riding around for pleasure once and the 50% who had done so twice or more do their "joy riding" with friends or relatives. With regard to the movies a full two-thirds had not gone to the downtown area in the previous two months. These activity data suggest, on the whole, that these black respondents make very few ventures into the broader urban community. Moreover, the previously cited data on participation in local community associations, with the exception of church contacts, confirm this picture of general non-contact with a variety of secondary organizations.

The data on metropolitan ventures indicate that these black respondents seldom venture beyond the household for the types of recreational activities indicated. Many factors undoubtedly enter into this phenomenon, including their relatively low incomes, their typically large families, their locality orientation, and fear of discrimination. Be that as it may, further light is shed on this restriction of travel to the Roxbury area by related data on commercial trips (Table 5:2). The data indicate that a substantial majority of these housewives have not gone on a business or medical trip in the last two to four weeks. Nearly one-tenth have not even gotten out for grocery shopping, and one-fifth have not ventured out for other types of shopping. Those who do go out seem to confine their shopping predominantly to the black ghetto, i. e., their local community. About 40% of all respondents making medical trips limit them to the Roxbury area ghetto. Approximately two-thirds of all respondents making business trips made them within the Roxbury area. Only in regard to other shopping, such as shopping for clothing or furniture, do Roxbury area residents seem to travel beyond the local ghetto area very often. Moreover, the overwhelming majority of respondents (77%) confine their grocery shopping to the local area. These figures are roughly comparable to the ones presented by Foley,[8] except that grocery shopping is not quite as confined for the Boston respondents.

TABLE 5:2

PERCENTAGE OF RESPONDENTS TAKING CERTAIN TYPES
OF TRIPS TO DESIGNATED AREAS OF BOSTON
BOSTON SAMPLE (N=120)

Part of Boston	Grocery Shopping[a]	Other Shopping[b]	Business Trips[b]	Medical Trips[b]
No Trips	9.2%	20.8%	79.1%	65.8%
Trips to				
Roxbury Only	60.8	22.5	14.2	9.2
Roxbury and Contiguous Area Only (South End, Jamaica Plain, Dorchester)	15.8	3.3	0.0	6.7
Downtown Only	0.0	35.0	3.3	4.2
Suburbs Only	6.7	5.8	0.0	5.0
Combinations of Above Areas and/or Other Places	7.5	12.6	3.4	9.1
Total	100.0%	100.0%	100.0%	100.0%

[a]The time period specified was "in the last two weeks."

[b]The time period specified was "in the last month."

The data, at least for these black women, refute the argument that the local area is of little importance to urban dwellers. Of course, these respondents are also discriminated against; but the pull of the local community even on white residents is testified to by the Foley study. There is no reason to suppose that black Americans are unlike other urbanites in this respect. And, in general, the restriction of most recreational and commercial trips to the locality jibes with the encapsulation of friendship, kinship, and associational ties indicated in previous chapters.

Little data specifically on the habits of black families vis-a-vis any of the mass media seem to be available as of the mid-1960s. Newspaper reading on the part of urbanites, largely white urbanites, has been a subject for investigation by numerous researchers. Such studies can provide a few points of reference for analyzing the Roxbury area findings. Bogart reports one study which showed that daily newspaper reading is extensive among U.S. citizens, regardless of their education. Daily reading was the rule for 53% of grade school graduates, 65% of high school graduates, and 77% of the college educated.[9] Another investigator collected extensive data on local newspapers and readers in Chicago. Indicating by their mere existence the vitality of local communities in a sprawling metropolis, such local papers numbered eighty-two in Chicago in 1950.[10] Janowitz argues persuasively that these papers, and other urban mass media as well, have contributed substantially to what concensus and social integration do exist in urban areas. "Mass media contributed to the growth of urban centers by providing the channels of integration and symbolism required for the integration and social solidarity of vast aggregates of the population."[11] Locally speaking, Chicago community papers provide one of the mechanisms for community integration. Only 16% of his subjects were non-readers; a minority (11%) were heavily committed fans. Community press readership correlated positively with high levels of exposure to city-wide mass media, including the metropolitan newspapers.[12] Tables 5:3 and 5:4 give, for the whole Roxbury area sample, the percent reading a metropolitan newspaper and the percent reading the local ghetto tabloid.

TABLE 5:3

CONTACT WITH MASS MEDIA: CITY-WIDE NEWSPAPERS (DAILIES)
BOSTON SAMPLE (N=120)

Frequency of Reading	Percentage of Respondents
Every day	64.2%
Several times a week	14.2
Once a week or less often	15.8
Not at all	5.0
Other answer/No answer	.8
Total	100.0%

The percentage of the black respondents who read the Boston papers daily is similar to the figure which Bogart found for a general sample of high school graduates (65%); indeed, they do not appear to differ greatly from other urbanites of roughly their same educational level. A comparison of Table 5:3 with Table 5:4 reveals that in regard to regularity of newspaper reading the sample is substantially more cosmopolitan-oriented than locally-oriented. Nearly two-thirds are regular readers of the metropolitan dailes, while only a quarter are regular readers of the two local weeklies. In fact, although only six respondents never read the metropolitan papers, forty-six do not read the local tabloids.

TABLE 5:4

CONTACT WITH MASS MEDIA: LOCAL ROXBURY NEWSPAPERS (WEEKLIES)
BOSTON SAMPLE (N=120)

Frequency of Reading	Percentage of Respondents
Once a week or more often	25.8%
Every few weeks or less often	35.0
Not at all	38.3
Other answer/No answer	.8
Total	99.9%

Every week the Roxbury City-News devotes its fifteen to twenty pages to news of the local ghetto. Organizational and social life reports often dominate, particularly on the activities of local civil rights and church-related organizations. The newspaper is middle-class in orientation and has been relatively militant in the local controversy against the Boston School Committee. Still, our findings suggest that it does not reach nearly as large a proportion of the local community as do the white-controlled and white-oriented metropolitan newspapers. Janowitz's finding that local paper readership tends to vary directly with attention to broader community media is corroborated by the Roxbury area data. The proportion of respondents who read the Boston paper daily rises as one goes from the group which does not read the local paper at all to the group which reads it weekly. This seems to support a cumulative hypothesis: as contact increases in one sphere, it also tends to increase in another. This general hypothesis will be examined in some detail in the next chapter.

TABLE 5:5

LOCAL PAPER READERSHIP BY CITY PAPER READERSHIP[a]
BOSTON SAMPLE (N=118)

| Boston Paper | Local Roxbury Paper | | | | | |
| | Never Read | | Read Occasionally | | Read Weekly | |
	Percent	N	Percent	N	Percent	N
Read Occasionally of Less Often	46.7%	(21)	35.7%	(15)	16.1%	(5)
Read Daily	53.3	(24)	64.3	(27)	83.9	(26)
Total	100.0%	(45)	100.0%	(42)	100.0%	(31)

$x^2 = 7.58$ p $<.05$.

64

TABLE 5:5 (cont.)

[a]For this and all subsequent tables which relate to questions of association between two variables the chi-square statistic has been calculated and appended. "No response" codes have usually been omitted.

What about the salience of newspaper reading? One section of the interview recorded the amount of time which respondents spent reading newspapers and magazines. When looked at this way, 79% of the sample did not read long enough for it to register when they were asked to give a time budget account of their day in fifteen-minute intervals. In this regard newspaper reading is apparently less significant than TV watching.

The importance of television viewing and radio listening for most Americans has been documented in numerous studies, although the former has been increasing at the expense of the latter. De Grazia, Meyersohn, Graham, and Komarovsky have reported that TV is the leisure-time activity in which Americans most frequently indulge.[13] Sweetser's study of TV watching for a general sample of Bostonians (usually mothers) revealed that nine-tenths of his respondents reduced the time devoted to radio listening when they bought a TV set; a substantial proportion also cut down on time spent at the movies, time with friends, and/or time reading.[14] The varying impact of television on individual opinions and behavior has also been testified to in several studies.[15] Most important to this thesis is the contention of Horton and Wohl that television gives the illusion of face-to-face social relationships with the performer(s):

> The media present opportunities for the playing of roles to which the spectator has -- or feels he has -- a legitimate claim, but for which he finds no opportunity in his social environment. This function of para-social then can properly be called compensatory, inasmuch as it provides the socially and psychologically isolated with a chance to enjoy the elixir of sociability.[16]

Commenting on the media and normal individuals, Horton and Wohl emphasize the significance of the mass media for the exploration of new roles. For most people the para-social complements normal social interactions; it reaffirms the assumptions and norms of everyday primary contacts. Yet for those deprived of primary contacts the media may have a vicarious function. The extent of this covariation will be examined in the next chapter.

For a general sample of the U. S. population Meyersohn reports that the average time watching TV per day, per person, is one hour and forty-five minutes.[17] This was also the figure for persons aged eighteen to fifty, the approximate range of ages in the Roxbury area sample. A paper by Sweetser, analyzing data collected in the Boston SMSA, reports a somewhat higher figure than this. For respondents aged twenty-one and over he found, on the average, two hours and thirty-one minutes of television watching daily. The blue-collar mothers in his sample reported an average of two hours and forty-seven minutes a day, a figure somewhat higher than for the sample as a whole.[18] In his book, The People Look at Television, Steiner reports that education correlated

negatively with television viewing. He found that those with zero to eight years
of education spent an average of 4.3 hours a day before "the tube"; the comparable
figure for high school graduates was 4.2 hours. For those with some college
education the figure was 2.9 hours daily.[19] The discrepancies between these
three studies are quite substantial and may be due to the fact that Steiner's
sample excludes non-viewers. However, two points do seem to be clear. First,
the less well educated and blue-collar respondents spend the most time watching
television; and second, the amount of time spent by the Bostonians and Steiner's
sample in all categories averaged more than two and one-half hours a day.

Included among the diverse questions asked of the black women in our
Boston sample was a time budget schedule. This required the respondent to
detail her dominant activities for each of seventy-two fifteen-minute time segments
from 6 A.M. until midnight; the day asked for was "yesterday" (or the last
week day). In addition, she was asked "from when to when" she did any subsidiary
activities. This question was particularly important in regard to the mass
media, since most occasionally carry out multiple activities, such as "eat
and watch TV," "sew and watch TV," etc. This method of detailing one's time
seems to be more reliable than asking "how much time do you spend daily," as
several studies have done. The data for the Roxbury area sample are quite
striking (Table 5:6). About 68% of these respondents had spent one and one-
quarter hours or more before the TV set on the last weekday preceding the
interview. A full 42.5% had thus spent three and one-quarter hours or more.
For a majority of the respondents this time spent watching TV was a major
activity at the time of viewing, that is, no other activities were listed
as going on at the same time. The mean amount of time watching TV for these
women was about two hours and fifty-four minutes; this figure is very close to
that which Sweetser found for his blue-collar whites in Boston. It is substantially greater than the figure which Meyersohn quotes for a national survey
completed several years ago, and a bit less than that which Steiner reports for
his grade school and high school graduates.

TABLE 5:6

PERCENTAGE OF RESPONDENTS SPENDING TIME WITH MASS MEDIA
BOSTON SAMPLE (N=120)

Mass Media Contact	Quarter Hours Spent in Contact (Time Budget Day)			
	0-4	5-12	13 or More	Total
Watching TV	32.5%	25.0	42.5	100.0%
Listening to Radio	76.7%	12.5	10.8	100.0%
Reading Newspaper or Magazine	95.0%	5.0	0.0	100.0%
Total Contact with Mass Media	18.3%	25.0	66.7	100.0%

The lesser significance of radio listening for typical respondents, noted by Bogart and Graham, also seems to be borne out by the Roxbury area data.[20] The mean amount of time spent listening to the radio was about fifty-four minutes daily. For the weekday specified by the interviewer, nearly 70% of the sample reported that they had not listened to the radio at all.

The summary data indicate that two-thirds of these black respondents spent three and one-quarter (or more) hours in contact with the four types of mass media (radio, TV, magazines, newspapers). Of this time TV watching was by far the largest consumer. Needless to say, the mass media are important in the lives of black women.

However, the degree of _significance_, particularly in the para-social sphere suggested by Horton and Wohl, of the media for these respondents is unknown. The impression one gets from reading our detailed interview schedules is that the TV (or radio) is, on occasion, _only a backdrop_ for other household acti-vities. And it may also be the case that TV watching is often a sociability arena for black Americans, just as it was in a study of Italians in the West End section of Boston.[21] Gans found that primary groups ("peer groups") composed mainly of relatives often congregated around the TV set, selectively admiring and ridiculing what was going on. For black Americans this important issue has yet to be investigated.

Another type of contact with the mass media takes the form of reading books. De Grazia found that 18% of his sample had done some book reading "yesterday," devoting on the average some forty-two minutes to this activity and to the reading of magazines.[22] Meyersohn reports that from 27% to 31% (depending on age) of the high school graduates in one sample had read a book in the last month.[23] In striking contrast, nearly two-thirds of the black respondents in the Roxbury area sample had done some reading in a book at least once in the last two months. Replying to a question "How many times have you read a book in the last two months?" nearly one-third said "once or twice." Another one-third had read a book from three to twenty-one times in the last two months. The data on activities, noted in the first part of this chapter, indicate the importance of movies, another type of mass media, in the lives of the black respondents. Several studies have indicated that movies are now the least important of the mass media for the average adult; for example, Berger found that only 15% of his working-class sample attended movies very often.[24] At least in regard to downtown movies two-thirds of the Roxbury area sample had not been out to see a movie in the last two months. If this were also true for the local theaters, it would be clear that the TV, the radio, the newspaper, and even books are much more important in the lives of these relatively low-income black Americans than Hollywood's films.

Conclusion

Several issues concerning more tenuous forms of integration into the urban social fabric have been considered in this chapter. The declining social significance of the local community within urban areas has been posited by some students of urban life. In general, Foley's research contradicts this argument and bespeaks an alternative position: that for certain given types of tertiary participation, such as commercial and recreational excursions, the use of local facilities is quite predominant. This substantiated contention makes even more sense when applied to a black community which is concentrated in one area of an urban complex, since residents of that sub-community are also hemmed in by discrimination.

Looking at the Boston data on black urbanites, the general tendency to use local facilities was found in the data indicating few recreational and commercial trips beyond the general Roxbury area. These findings tend to confirm a picture of social encapsulation, although one must not exaggerate this generalization. The overall impression is one of few trips <u>at all</u>, beyond grocery and other shopping excursions. On the whole, this type of social activity does indeed seem to be of lesser significance than other types of social activity, at least for these women in relatively large blue-collar families.

The mass media provide tenuous links between persons in urban areas, at least in the sense of para-social ties and subliminal interaction. That the mass media have become a habit for most urbanites is borne out in several research studies. Comparisons with data on other black samples are generally not possible in this area of mass media contact, as well as in the area of empirical studies of local facility use. In comparison with some findings on white samples, however, the Boston women do not appear to be greatly different. They tend to read newspapers, watch TV, and see movies about as often as whites do -- particularly those whites who are most comparable in occupational status. The previous data indicating relatively strong primary ties, together with these findings of normal media contact, also argue against a contention that some students of ghettos and slums might well make: that being isolated from primary contacts would force them into spending an unusual amount of time absorbed in the mass media.

68

FOOTNOTES

(Chapter V)

[1]Technically speaking, these trips are often made to "secondary" organizations, such as businesses and libraries. The point in calling them "tertiary" is to suggest that they are not as significant in the average individual's social life as the type of "secondary" tie examined in the last chapter, i.e., participation in voluntary organizations.

[2]Vide Stein, op. cit., p. 329.

[3]Greer, The Emerging City, loc. cit.; and Bell and Boat, op. cit.

[4]Donald L. Foley, "The Use of Local Facilities in a Metropolis," Cities and Society, eds. Paul K. Hatt and Albert J. Reiss, Jr. (New York: The Free Press of Glencoe, 1957), p. 607.

[5]Ibid., p. 613.

[6]Ibid., p. 611.

[7]Svend Riemer and John McNamara, "Contact Patterns in the City," Social Forces, 36 (1957), pp. 137ff.

[8]Foley, op. cit., p. 611.

[9]Leo Bogard, "The Mass Media and the Blue-Collar Worker," Blue-Collar World, eds. Arthur B. Shostak and William Gomberg (Englewood Cliffs, New Jersey: Prentice-Hall, Inc., 1964), p. 624. Sex of respondents is not specified by the studies cited by Bogart.

[10]Morris Janowitz, The Community Press in an Urban Setting (Glencoe, Illinois: Free Press, 1952), p. 16.

[11]Ibid.

[12]Ibid., pp. 208-212. Janowitz' sample included men and women.

[13]Sebastian de Grazia, "The Uses of Time," Aging and Leisure, ed. Robert W. Kleemeier (New York: Oxford University Press, 1961), p. 121; Rolf Meyersohn, "A Critical Examination of Commercial Entertainment," Aging and Leisure, ed. Robert W. Kleemeier (New York: Oxford University Press, 1961), pp. 264ff; Saxon Graham, "Social Correlates of Adult Leisure-Time Behavior," Community Structure and Analysis, ed. Marvin B. Sussman (New York: Thomas Y. Crowell, 1959), p. 339; and Mirra Komarovsky, Blue-Collar Marriage (New York: Random House, 1962), p. 324.

[14]Frank L. Sweetser, Jr., "Home Television and Behavior: Some Tentative Conclusions," Public Opinion Quarterly, 19 (1955), 79-84.

[15]Gary Steiner, The People Look at Television (New York: Alfred A. Knopf, Inc. 1963).

[16]D. Horton and R. R. Wohl, "Mass Media and Para-Social Interaction," Psychiatry, 3 (1956), p. 222.

[17]Meyersohn, op. cit., pp. 266f.

[18]Sweetser, op. cit., pp. 80f.

[19]Steiner, op. cit., p. 75.

[20]Bogart, op. cit., p. 421; and Graham, op. cit., p. 339.

[21]Gans, op. cit., pp. 188-192.

[22]de Grazia, op. cit., p. 124.

[23]Meyersohn, op. cit., p. 263.

[24]Berger, op. cit., p. 117. Cf. Graham, op. cit., pp. 339ff.

CHAPTER VI

THE RELATIONSHIPS BETWEEN SOCIAL INTEGRATION INDICES

Up to this point three major areas of social integration have been examined. Looking at primary, secondary, and tertiary social ties, I have detailed the extent to which these black Bostonians are integrated into the social phenomenon which is the city. In the area of primary ties the extensity and intensity of friendship, neighboring, and kinship have been investigated; the area of secondary participation was examined in terms of ties to voluntary associations. The tertiary area, admittedly a potpourri, was delineated in terms of such measures as excursions into the city and contact with the mass media. This chapter will concentrate on certain important types of covariation between indices from each of these three participation areas.

Why is the examination of covariation important? Basic to the issues here are several hypotheses about the whole area of social contact which have been hinted at by several authors cited in earlier chapters. For example, Lundberg and his associates have argued for a "lump of sociability" hypothesis:

If we assume that there is a limit to emotional or social expan-
siveness, it is to be expected that as the number of contacts increase, at least beyond a certain point, their intensity decreases.[1]

This suggests the hypothesis that extensity and intensity should vary inversely: that is, the more individuals contacted in one's social rounds, the weaker the intensity of the socio-emotional bond with each individual. Lundberg extends this conception from the number of individuals and mean intensity per individual to the idea of covariation between different areas of socia-bility. On the one hand, it may be that the diffusion of one's energies among primary attachments decreases the possibility of (and/or weakens the intensity of) one's bonds with secondary groups, such as voluntary associa-tions. Or, on the other hand, a person active in such voluntary associations is not likely to "cultivate as intense, self-sufficient and narrow friendships as the person who devotes all his emotional and social energies to primary group interaction."[2]

Caplow, Stryker, and Wallace have suggested a different hypothesis about neighboring intensity and extensity, one which is incompatible with the "lump of sociability" view. This is what they call the "Rotarian" hypothesis, which can be generalized beyond neighboring as follows; there will be a positive correlation between activity in one area of social interaction and activity in another.[3] A person who is very active, for example, in voluntary associations is likely to have more close friends (or more primary relationships) than someone who is not so active. Several studies of rural areas suggest that there is just such a relationship between associa-tional membership and neighborhood activity,[4] as do a few studies of middle-class suburbs.[5] Moreover, such a hypothesis points to another: a person who is active in secondary associations and has numerous primary contacts also will have more tertiary (tenuous social or parasocial) contacts, such as excursions into the city, book and newspaper reading, and even TV watching. And according to the "Rotarian" hypothesis those less active in one area of participation tend to be less active in other areas.

In part, the following discussion will examine the applicability of these two contrasting hypotheses to several types of covariation, some of which have arisen as side issues in previous chapters. Data from several sources will be compared with the Boston findings.[6]

Extensity and Intensity: Primary Contacts

In a San Juan study Caplow, Stryker, and Wallace found that families who had a high intensity of neighboring interaction were likely to associate with few neighbors; and, in general, the mean interaction intensity declined as the number of relationships increased.[7] This lends support for one version of the "lump of sociability" hypothesis. Further examination indicated another striking phenomenon: "A family which widens its circle of acquaintances may hope to increase the number of friends, but the increment of friendship, so to speak, is less than proportionate to each added increment of acquaintanceship."[8] Thus, as the number of neighbors visited increases, the decline in mean intensity occurs because of a decline in the proportion of higher intensity relationships, not because of the decreasing number of intimate ties.

Since our neighboring data are not of a kind which can be used to test the Caplow finding in regard to neighboring, it is best to look at our data on other kinds of informal association, i.e., interaction with friends and kin. The table for kin revealed that respondents with many relatives were just as likely as respondents with few relatives to have a high mean intensity of contact per relative; this similarity also held up at low and medium mean intensity of contact. On the one hand, the number of relatives seen seems to have little effect on the mean intensity of contact for the Boston respondents. On the other hand, Table 6:1 conveys the impression that there is some coincident variation between the number of friends a respondent has and her mean frequency of interacting with those friends.

TABLE 6:1

NUMBER OF FRIENDS SEEN BY MEAN INTENSITY OF CONTACT
BOSTON SAMPLE (N=116)

| Mean Intensity Score Per Friend | Number of Friends | | | | | |
| | Few (0-2) | | Many (3-14) | | Total | |
	Percent	N	Percent	N	Percent	N
Low[a] (0-4.0)	37.7%	(20)	31.7%	(20)	34.5%	(40)
Medium (4.1-5.0)	32.1%	(17)	50.8	(32)	42.2%	(49)
High (5.1-6.0)	30.1%	(16)	17.5	(11)	23.3%	(27)
Total	99.9%	(53)	100.0%	(63)	100.0%	(116)

$x^2 = 4.691.$ p $<$ .10.

[a]"Low," "medium" and "high" breaks in this and subsequent tables were made at the (possible) points on the variable which best divided the set of scores into thirds. The bunching of respondents at some points allows only an approximation of thirds.

About 30% of those with zero to two friends fall into the highest mean intensity level (upper third), as compared with 17.5% of those who have three to fourteen friends. At the other end of the spectrum, however, there is a 6% difference between those with few and those with many friends, but the difference is in the same direction; that is, the lowest level of intensity draws a greater percentage of those with few friends than of those with many friends. There is a somewhat greater tendency for those with larger numbers of friends to fall into the medium range of average contact than those with few friends. Thus the "lump of sociability" hypothesis is given a little support by the finding that a larger proportion of those with few friends than those with many friends, had a high mean interaction score. It may well be that the percentage distribution for those with many friends hides a phenomenon similar to that which Caplow et al. found in regard to neighboring: a decline in mean intensity because of a decline in the proportion (not the number) of more intimate ties.

Primary Covariation

Investigating neighboring patterns, researchers have found that neighbors on occasion become close friends. Approximately one-third of the friendships of urbanites seem to be due to mere propinquity.[9] This certainly suggests that there should be some positive association between neighboring in general and friendship contacts. Data from a study by Smith, Form, and Stone indicate that respondents in areas of more intensive neighboring are more likely to draw friends from that area than those who live in areas with less local intimacy of this type.[10] This finding also suggests that the "Rotarian" hypothesis holds for friendship and neighboring, i.e., that there should be a positive correlation between neighboring and friendship. To my knowledge, no one has yet examined this question for black respondents. The working-class status of the Boston sample might lead one to expect lower levels of neighboring than have been found in middle-class areas; however, in a previous chapter it was found that they do a fair amount of neighboring, roughly comparable to that found for white samples. Thus, there seems to be little reason not to predict a positive association of neighboring and friendship contact for the Boston sample. This expectation is confirmed by the data (Table 6:2). On the one hand, 60% of the respondents who interact most extensively with friends also have a high level of neighboring, while only 10% of these same subjects have a quite low level of neighboring.

TABLE 6:2

FRIENDSHIP CONTACT BY NEIGHBORING
BOSTON SAMPLE (N=119)

Total Neighboring Score	Friendship Contact (Total Intensity Score)							
	Low		Medium		High		Total	
	Percent	N	Percent	N	Percent	N	Percent	N
Low	57.9%	(22)	46.3%	(19)	10.0%	(4)	37.8%	(45)
Medium	26.3%	(10)	22.0	(9)	30.0	(12)	26.1%	(31)
High	15.8%	(6)	31.7	(13)	60.0	(24)	36.1%	(43)
Total	100.0%	(38)	100.0%	(41)	100.0%	(40)	100.0%	(119)

$x^2 = 24.41.$ p <.001.

There is a very strong tendency for blacks with a high level of friendship contact to have a high level of neighboring contact. On the other hand, about 58% of those with a relatively low level of friendship interaction also fall into the lowest third in degree of neighboring, while only 16% of these same subjects fall into the highest level of neighboring. This positive relationship between friendship and neighboring holds at about the same level, when visiting with neighbors is plotted against the friendship intensity scores. In general, these results strongly support the cumulative or "Rotarian" hypothesis.

In regard to primary covariation another issue has been raised directly or indirectly by several researchers: the relationship of kin contact to friend contact. A logical hypothesis suggested by the zero-sum point of view would be: individuals with a lot of intimate friends will have less contact with relatives than people with few friends. Commenting on his kin-oriented working-class respondents, Berger has argued that friends can serve as the functional equivalent of kin particularly for upwardly mobile (middle-class) nuclear families.[11] He provides no data for this contention. Conversely, this general point of view might lead one to expect that individuals with a lot of kin contact will interact with fewer friends than those with little kin contact. Only a few studies shed much light on this particular relationship, and apparently only one specifically deals with these hypotheses. Bott's intensive case studies of twenty British families do furnish some hints that families with less intimate (or no) kin contacts make up for them by intimate friendship ties.[12] However, an East London study suggests that, at the other end of the spectrum, those with extensive kinship ties do not decrease the extent of their friendship interaction; in fact "those most sociable inside the family were also the most sociable outside."[13] Yet two-thirds of their respondents did not exchange visits with any friends.

Babchuk has specifically investigated the aforementioned hypotheses, one of which he states as follows: "Couples who have more extensive and frequent contact with kin will visit with primary friends less frequently."[14] His statistical data, however, give no support to this hypothesis. In general, the pattern is one of no correlation; those with no, few, or many kin contacts were equally likely to have extensive contacts with friends.[15] Although none of these studies have been done on Negro families in a ghetto area, there seems little reason not to predict, following Babchuk's empirical study, a random relationship between kin contact and friend contact for the Roxbury area sample. Looking at the data in Table 6:3 reveals little or no association between the two variables. Those housewives with high levels of frienship contact are no more likely than those with low levels of friendship contact to have a high degree of contact with relatives. In fact, the table essentially supports a random distribution hypothesis of no, linear or curvilinear, relationship between these two measures of primary group participation. Knowing the extent of kinship contact for an individual black adult tells us nothing about friendship contacts. This finding corresponds to that which Babchuk found for his white couples.

TABLE 6:3

FRIENDSHIP CONTACT BY CONTACT WITH RELATIVES
BOSTON SAMPLE (N=120)

Contact With Relatives	Contact With Friends							
	Low		Medium		High		Total	
	Percent	N	Percent	N	Percent	N	Percent	N
Low	42.1%	(16)	31.8%	(13)	34.1%	(14)	35.8%	(43)
Medium	26.3%	(10)	34.1	(14)	31.8	(13)	30.8%	(37)
High	31.6%	(12)	34.1	(14)	34.1	(14)	33.3%	(40)
Total	100.0%	(38)	100.0%	(41)	100.0%	(41)	99.9%	(120)

$x^2 = 1.10$. n.s.

Primary and Tertiary Covariation

Turning from an internal analysis of primary integration into urban social life, we can move into the area of covariation between the different types of social integration: primary to secondary, secondary to tertiary, and primary to tertiary. First, the question of the relationship between a main type of tertiary interaction, mass media contact, and primary interaction will be examined. Various studies of radio and TV have pointed out the para-social function(s) which the mass media can have in the lives of those weakly integrated into social groups. The Rileys have engaged in research upon the social integration of children.[16] Some children were found to have weak primary ties with others; in a compensatory reaction they came to the radio and other mass media looking for fantasy and escape, while children who were better integrated judged the media in terms of its contributions to group life. This is essentially the argument of Horton and Wohl in their stimulating article on "Mass Communication and Para-social Interaction."[17] They point out that the mass media, particularly TV, can provide compensatory social relationships for the socially isolated, the socially inept, the timid, or the aged. Many mass media personalities and their directors are quite aware of this compensatory relationship and intentionally play the "persona" for the isolated. "Most characteristic is the attempt of the persona to duplicate the gestures, conversational style, and milieu of an informal face-to-face gathering."[18]

This suggests the following hypothesis: respondents who are isolated from friendship and kinship networks will rely more extensively upon the mass media for communication and socio-emotional reasons than those who are not isolated. Sweetser suggests, on the basis of his research, that this hypothesis holds up in reverse fashion, i.e., some of those who watch the TV a lot (for whatever reason), inevitably have to cut down on visiting friends.[19] Such a position is essentially proposing a variation of the general "lump of sociability" hypothesis: people have so much time for sociability and time spent in para-social interaction cuts down on time available for social interaction. Combining friendship and kinship interaction scores to get a general primary interaction measure, I plotted these new scores against the measure of mass media interaction (radio, newspaper, TV, and magazines) gleaned from the Roxbury area respondents' "yesterday" time budgets. The figures in Table 6:4 do not offer support for the hypothesis. There is no significant tendency for those who are more isolated from primary social contacts to spend more time with the mass media. The compensatory theory is not borne out. In fact, those in the lowest primary contact group also had the largest percentage at the low mass media contact level (41%). In addition, separate tables for friendship-mass media, and kinship-mass media were also tabulated. In neither case does a significant association occur. Thus, there is evidence neither for a "lump of sociability" hypothesis nor for a "Rotarian" hypothesis in regard to this particular type of primary-tertiary covariation.

For the great majority of the mass media audience, Horton and Wohl have emphasized, the para-social is complementary to normal social interaction. "It provides the social milieu in which the every day assumptions and understandings of primary group interaction and sociability are demonstrated and re-affirmed."[20] A more adequate statement of the situation might be the reverse.

TABLE 6:4

INFORMAL SOCIAL PARTICIPATION (FRIEND-KIN) BY MASS MEDIA CONTACT
BOSTON SAMPLE (N=120)

Mass Media Contact (One Day)	Informal Social Participation (Primary)							
	Low		Medium		High		Total	
	Percent	N	Percent	N	Percent	N	Percent	N
Low (0-2 hours)	41.0%	(16)	30.0%	(12)	26.8%	(11)	32.5%	(39)
Medium (2¼-4½ hours)	25.6%	(10)	37.5	(15)	39.0	(16)	34.2%	(41)

(Table 6:4 continued on next page)

Table 6:4, Informal Social Participation (Friend-Kin) by Mass Media Contact (Cont.)

	Percent	N	Percent	N	Percent	N	Percent	N
High (4 3/4-15¾ hours)	33.3%	(13)	32.5	(13)	34.1	(14)	33.3%	(40)
Total	99.9%	(39)	100.0%	(40)	99.9%	(41)	100.0%	(120)

x^2 = 2.61. n.s.

That is, primary groups provide the social milieu within which the majority of Americans receive the messages of the media. This fact has been testified to by a few studies. Notable is the finding that Italians in the West End of Boston enjoyed the media, but largely within kin-based peer groups which filtered out whatever was alien to the values of the group.[21] Katz and Lazarsfeld also testify to this point in their study of personal influence.[22] The evidence from the Roxbury area study does not, at least, contradict these contentions about the relationship between primary groups and the mass media. Table 6:4 indicates that, regardless of the level of primary integration, approximately one-third of the subjects spend a quite substantial amount of time -- over four and three-quarters hours -- with the mass media. Another two-thirds at each level of informal integration spend a more moderate amount of time in contact with the media; and the overwhelming majority of the sample spend some time in contact with the various media. The question which is crucial here is the function which the TV, radio, newspaper, or magazine plays in the lives of those who are (or are not) social isolates. This question cannot be answered from the Roxbury area data, although further analysis of the time budget schedules may reveal the social setting(s) in which respondents had contact with the mass media.

Secondary and Primary Covariation

So far I have raised several questions about primary and tertiary contacts. What about the relation of secondary affiliation and primary interaction? Or secondary association and mass media contact? The first question is one which has been intimated by numerous observers and has been openly asked by a few researchers. Axelrod's important study of urban social structure in Detroit indicated that the number of primary contacts were associated positively with membership in formal associations. Cumulating contacts with friends, relatives, and neighbors for a two-month period he found that those with thirteen or more such contacts were more likely to hold membership in formal associations than those with twelve or fewer such contacts.[23] Over two-thirds of those in the "13 contacts or more" bracket, as opposed to 44% of those in the "0-4 contacts" bracket belonged to at least one voluntary association. No breakdown is indicated by extent of formal association, beyond this yes-no dichotomy, nor is any evidence presented on the issue of neighboring and associational membership or friendship and membership.

Bell and Boat present some brief evidence on this question of friendship and associational membership; they suggest that attendance at associational meetings in the area brings men together in inter-personal contacts which can be primary in nature. Over 51% of associational members in each of their low-status and high-status neighborhoods reported that they had several friends who were also members of the same associations.[24] "Thus most individuals find the formal association by no means as impersonal as is often assumed."[25] Similarly, Hay found, for a sample of 138 rural households, that the extent of formal association membership correlated +.52 with the number of family friendships.[26] Citing evidence from their Lincoln, Nebraska study, Babchuk and Thompson have presented some of the relatively little available data on the covariation of social participation for black adults. In their sample of 120 adult males and females a strong positive correlation between associational membership and the number of intimate friends turned up.[27] About 40% of those who held four or more memberships in associations reported six or more friends, as compared with 17% of those with one to three memberships and 13% of those with zero memberships. All of the foregoing studies therefore support a "Rotarian" hypothesis: friendship interaction will vary directly with associational activity for both black and white adults.

Table 6:5 shows the cross-tabulation of associational participation with levels of friendship interaction for the Roxbury area sample. The data corroborate the aforementioned studies of whites. The hypothesis of a positive correlation between friendship, one major type of primary social integration, and associational activity is borne out. About 58% of those women with a high degree of associational participation also had a high level of friendship interaction, while only one-fifth of those with little or no associational contact had a high level of friendship contact. The other end of the spectrum appears as expected: 11% of those who have high associational participation and 43% of those who have low associational participation fall into the lowest third on the distribution of friendship contact intensity.

Several rural studies have turned up evidence that neighboring activity is positively correlated with participation in voluntary associations.

TABLE 6:5

ASSOCIATIONAL PARTICIPATION BY FRIENDSHIP CONTACT
BOSTON SAMPLE (N=120)

Friendship Contact Intensity	Associational Participation							
	Low		Medium		High		Total	
	Percent	N	Percent	N	Percent	N	Percent	N
Low	42.5%	(17)	40.5%	(17)	10.5%	(4)	31.7%	(38)
Medium	37.5%	(15)	33.3	(14)	31.6	(12)	34.2%	(41)
High	20.0%	(8)	26.2	(11)	57.9	(22)	34.2%	(41)
Total	100.0%	(40)	100.0%	(42)	100.0%	(38)	100.1%	(120)

$x^2 = 17.48.$ $p < .01.$

For example, in an article entitled "The Behavioral Correlates of Membership in Rural Neighborhoods" Christiansen reports that neighboring correlates positively with extent of participation in a variety of types of rural associations.[28] This points to a "Rotarian" or cumulative hypothesis, similar to the one which holds between friendship and associational activities. Table 6:6 indicates the degree of relationship between neighborly interaction and associational participation for the Boston respondents. The evidence indicates a curvilinear relationship. It is the case that those with the highest association scores have the largest percentage in the upper third of the neighboring scores and the smallest percentage in the lower third. This would support the cumulative hypothesis. However, those with the largest percentage in the lower third of neighboring scores and the smallest percentage in the upper third are not the most infrequent associational participators. It is those at the medium level of associational participation who seem to do the least neighboring, while the least frequent participators fall in between the medium and high level participators on the spectrum of neighboring.

TABLE 6:6

NEIGHBORING BY ASSOCIATIONAL PARTICIPATION
BOSTON SAMPLE (N=119)

Total Neighboring Score (3-12)	Associational Participation							
	Low		Medium		High		Total	
	Percent	N	Percent	N	Percent	N	Percent	N
Low	40.0%	(16)	48.8%	(20)	23.7%	(9)	37.8%	(45)
Medium	25.0%	(10)	24.4	(10)	28.9	(11)	26.1%	(31)
High	35.0%	(14)	26.8	(11)	47.4	(18)	36.1%	(43)
Total	100.0%	(40)	100.0%	(41)	100.0%	(38)	100.0%	(119)

x^2 = 5.87. n.s.

Secondary and Tertiary Covariation

The cumulative or "Rotarian" hypothesis seems to be supported by the Roxbury area data on friendship interaction and partially by the data on neighboring. But what about the relationship between activity in voluntary associations and para-social participation in the mass media? The compensatory theory of the function of the mass media implies that there would be a negative association between participation in secondary groups and tertiary participation; this is another version of the "lump of sociability" hypothesis. Queen found this to be the case in his study; these two measures of social participation were negatively correlated.[29]

TABLE 6:7

ASSOCIATIONAL PARTICIPATION BY MASS MEDIA CONTACT
BOSTON   SAMPLE (N=120)

Mass Media Contact (One Day)	Associational Participation							
	Low		Medium		High		Total	
	Percent	N	Percent	N	Percent	N	Percent	N
Low	32.5%	(13)	35.7%	(15)	28.9%	(11)	32.5%	(39)
Medium	22.5%	(9)	26.2	(11)	55.3	(21)	34.2%	(41)
High	45.0%	(18)	38.1	(16)	15.8	(6)	33.3%	(40)
Total	100.0%	(40)	100.0%	(42)	100.0%	(38)	100.0%	(120)

$x^2 = 13.0.$ $p < .02.$

Although no research has yet been reported for a black sample, there seems to be little reason not to expect some negative association between the two for the Roxbury area sample. Observing the data, one readily sees that the relationship is a complex one. It is true that there is some evidence for the "lump of sociability" hypothesis. The high associational contact group does have the smallest percentage of the three associational groups falling into this high level, while the lowest associational group has a full 45% of its members falling into this high mass media bracket. This suggests that for some of the isolates from voluntary association activity the TV set, the radio, and/or the newspaper may be fulfilling a para-social function. However, those in the highest associational group also have the smallest percentage falling at the "little or no" mass media contact level; and compared to the other associational groups they have the largest percentage falling into the medium level of mass media contact. It seems that these respondents are more likely to watch TV or have contact with the mass media than the other associational levels, but are the least likely to spend a lot of time with the media. This suggests that there is some negative association between media contact and associational activity, particularly when a minimal level of contact is surpassed. It also lends support to the view, mentioned earlier, that the media are important in the lives of most normal people, operating in a complementary fashion and within a concrete social milieu.

Conclusion

In this relatively complex chapter I have analyzed certain hypotheses which have come up in regard to the relationship between the several types of social participation. These hypotheses have arisen in earlier discussions, here and elsewhere, of individual variables; and it seemed appropriate to combine them systematically in one chapter. Having summary measures from each of the three areas of participation on the same respondents, white or black, is a rarity in the literature. Examination of these relationships for the black sample in Boston's ghetto has revealed some interesting types of covariation and has shed some light on the social integration of these respondents. In summary:

1. Some evidence for each of the following "Rotarian" hypotheses (suggested in the literature) is provided by the data on the Boston sample:
   a) Friendship contact will correlate positively with neighboring.
   b) Frienship contact will correlate positively with associational participation.
   c) Associational participation will vary directly with neighboring (partially supported).
2. The following "lump of sociability" hypotheses (suggested by the literature) are generally not supported by the Boston findings:
   a) Informal interaction will correlate negatively with mass media contact.
   b) Friendship contact will correlate negatively with kin contact.
3. Evidence from the Boston data is provided for two qualified "lump of sociability" hypotheses (suggested by the literature):
   a) Associational participation will vary inversely with mass media contact, once a certain threshold level of media contact is exceeded.
   b) Mean intensity of friendship contact will correlate negatively with the number of friends a respondent has, once a certain threshold of interaction is surpassed.

The substantiated hypotheses in section one and the unsubstantiated hypotheses in section two argue against the general "lump of sociability" point of view, the view that respondents who participate actively in one area are forced to cut back on their activities in another area. At least this is not the case for these black women in relatively large, low-income and low-middle-income families. In general, there is some tendency for those who are more active in voluntary associations to maintain more active friendship and neighboring links; and it also seems to be the case that those who maintain very active friendship and neighboring ties are just as likely as others to have a certain minimal level of contact with the mass media and to maintain ties with their relatives. Those women who are not as active in associations tend to participate somewhat less widely in friendship and neighboring behavior, and at the lowest level of associational contact, to have greater than average contact with the mass media. The partial confirmation of hypothesis 3-b indicates that they may make up for this relative lack of extensive informal contacts by somewhat more intensive interaction with the friends and kin they do have.

One further point is in order. Hypothesis 2-b is not supported by the Roxbury area data. Those with a low level of friendship contact were just as likely as those with a high level of friendship contact to sustain regular interaction with their kin. This agrees with the general picture of non-isolation presented in Chapter III. Either kin or friends or both are important links into the social fabric of the city; and 97% of the respondents are integrated through these ties, either singly or in combination.

FOOTNOTES

(Chapter 6)

[1]George A. Lundberg and M. Steele, "Social Attraction Patterns in a Village," Sociometry, 1 (1938), p. 390.

[2]Ibid., p. 416.

[3]Caplow, Stryker, and Wallace, op. cit., p. 179.

[4]John R. Christiansen, "The Behavorial Correlates of Membership in Rural Neighborhoods," Rural Sociology, 22 (1957), 12-19. Cf. also Hubert F. Lionberger and Edward Hassinger, "Neighborhoods as a Factor in the Diffusion of Farm Information in a Northeast Missouri Farming Community," Rural Sociology, 19 (1954), 377-384.

[5]Seeley, Sim, and Loosley, op. cit.

[6]The following analysis will not examine all logical combinations of participation indices; I will concentrate on the more theoretically interesting relationships, all of which have been discussed directly or indirectly in the general literature on social participation. The number of relationships which it is possible to examine is also limited by the availability of a summary measure on the Boston Negro respondents.

[7]Caplow, Stryker, and Wallace, op. cit., p. 182.

[8]Ibid., p. 183.

[9]Vide Smith, Form, and Stone, op. cit., p. 277; and Bell and Boat, op. cit.

[10]Smith, Form, and Stone, op. cit., p. 279.

[11]Berger, op. cit., p. 68.

[12]Elizabeth Bott, Family and Social Network (London: Tavistock Publications, Ltd., 1959), pp. 76ff.

[13]Young and Willmont, op. cit., p. 108.

[14]Nicholas Babchuk, "Primary Friends and Kin: A Study of the Associations of Middle-Class Couples," Social Forces, 43 (1964-1965), 485.

[15]Ibid., p. 488.

[16]Matilda W. Riley and John W. Riley, Jr., "A Sociological Approach to Community Research," Public Opinion Quarterly, 15 (1951), 445-460.

85

[17]Horton and Wohl, op. cit.

[18]Ibid., p. 217.

[19]Sweetser, op. cit., p. 83.

[20]Horton and Wohl, op. cit., pp. 223f.

[21]Gans, op. cit., p. 194.

[22]Katz and Lazarsfeld, op. cit.

[23]Axelrod, op. cit., pp. 729f.

[24]Bell and Boat, op. cit., p. 397.

[25]Ibid., p. 398.

[26]Donald Hay, "A Scale for Measurement of Social Participation of Rural Households," Rural Sociology, 13 (1948), 285-294.

[27]Babchuk and Thompson, op. cit., p. 652.

[28]Christiansen, op. cit. Cf. also Lionberger and Hassinger, op. cit.

[29]Stuart A. Queen, "Social Participation in Relation to Social Disorganization," American Sociological Review, 14 (1949), 256f.

CHAPTER VII

INCOME, STATUS, AND SOCIAL PARTICIPATION

As indicated in Chapter II, the general sample upon which this analysis has
so far been based comprises three different housing and two different income
groups. It includes a low-income sample from public housing and two similar samples from the private market (movers and non-movers), a middle-income sample from
221 (d)3 housing in the Roxbury urban renewal area, and a sample of low-income
rent supplementation families also living in the same 221 (d)3 housing.[1] This
chapter and the one following will examine differences in social participation
among these samples, as well as analyze the effects of the move on each of the
four mobility samples. This chapter will focus specifically upon the social integration of these black families as it is influenced by their somewhat differing
socioeconomic status.

"Poverty" is an ambiguous term; different researchers and policy makers use
different definitions. Of particular importance is the breaking point on the income scale which one chooses. The Lampman report, a study paper of the Joint
Economic Committee of Congress, uses a poverty line of $2,500 (for a family of
four).[2] Keyserling and others have used a $4,000 level, sometimes relating this
to a family of four and sometimes not specifying family size.[3]

TABLE 7:1

DESCRIPTIVE STATISTICS ON LOW-INCOME AND MIDDLE-INCOME ADULT FEMALES[a]
BOSTON SAMPLE (N=120)

		Low-Income Group	Middle-Income Group
1.	Number	91	29
2.	Mean income	$3900	$5300
3.	Mean age of wife	33	33
4.	Mean number of children	4.7	4.0
5.	Percentage of female-headed families	50%	59%
6.	Percentage on welfare	33%	7%
7.	Mean education		
	Husband	9.7	11.2
	Wife	10.3	11.1
8.	Percentage of husbands in blue-collar positions	94%	80%

Table 7:1 Continued on next page

TABLE 7:1 CONTINUED

DESCRIPTIVE STATISTICS ON LOW-INCOME AND MIDDLE-INCOME ADULT FEMALES
BOSTON SAMPLE (N=120)

	Low-Income Group	Middle-Income Group
9. Percentage of wives considering themselves		
Lower class	20%	4%
Working class	53%	78%

aWith one exception the data in this table are taken from the "after-move" interviews; income figures are from administrative records. Since we were unable to get income figures on six of the low-income respondents, the figure given is based on an N of 85.

Whatever the defintion of poverty, the families in four of the Roxbury area subsamples are definitely at the lower end of the economic spectrum. For the private movers and the rent supplementation sample the mean incomes are approximately $4,500 and $4,100; the other two low-income samples, private non-movers and public housing, have mean incomes of $4,000 and $3,100. The mean income for the four combined samples is $3,900 per family; and the mean number of children per family is 4.7. In subsequent comparisons these subsamples combined will be considered as one large-family, low-income sample representing three different housing groups in the Boston Negro community. If the $4,000 for a family of four guideline is used, these families are well down into the poverty level.

Composed of twenty-nine economically better-off families, the non-subsidized tenants in the "middle-income" 221(d)3 projects will be used as a middle-income comparison group. Their mean income was substantially higher than for the low-income group. Yet it is lower than the national average for all families.[4] The exact figure, rounded to hundreds as in all the above figures, is $5,300.

Their mean family size, mean age of housewife, and percentage of female-headed families are roughly the same as for the low-income group, since the several housing groups were originally matched on those variables. Thus, they are a group of low-middle-income to middle-income families of relatively large size. Source of income is also an important variable; almost all of the middle-income families, 93% of them, are not receiving any public aid. Most do not receive aid, often considered non-respectable in the higher-status segments of the black community, from the federal and state welfare programs. One-third of the low-income families are at least partially dependent on public aid.

The two groups differ in regard to the education received by both husbands and wives. The lower-income housewives average nearly one grade lower in educational attainment than the middle-income group. The mean educational attainment for low-income wives is 10.3, while for middle-income respondents it is 11.1. For husbands the difference is a bit more. The mean educational attainment for middle-income husbands is 11.2, while for the low-income groups it is 1.5 grades less. One-fifth of the low-income wives reported that their husbands did not finish the eight grade; none of the middle-income husbands had less than an eighth grade education.

In addition to income and education, it is important to examine occupational differences between the two income groups. Unfortunately, no data on spouse's occupation are available for some of the female-based families; data on husband's occupation were secured from only 71 of the 120 families. One-fifth of the low-income husbands are employed in service or unskilled labor jobs, as compared with one-seventh of the middle-income sample. One-fifth of the middle-income husbands are employed in white-collar jobs, compared with 6% of those in the low-income sample. While none of the middle-income males are currently unemployed, one-seventh of the low-income husbands are out of work. However, the bulk (60-67%) of both samples are currently employed in stable blue-collar positions, as craftsmen, foremen, or operatives.

The low-income sample is composed of a larger number of poor families who face irregular economic circumstances. Although the employed husbands in both samples are predominantly blue-collar by occupational status, the middle-income families have somewhat higher and more stable incomes. This is because of their better paid blue-collar jobs and their wives, many of whom are employed part-time.

In regard to working wives the middle-income sample has a larger number employed than the low-income group. Only ten of the ninety-one low-income wives, as compared with sixteen of the twenty-nine middle-income wives, are currently employed. Undoubtedly, the fact that 55% of the middle-income wives are in the labor force accounts in part for their higher family incomes. Their ability to save, usually considered a characteristic of the middle classes, is illustrated by responses to the following question: "Are you saving any money right now?" This was followed by a question asking for what they were saving. Twenty-six of the 120 black wives indicated that they are saving for a house, their children's education, or emergencies. Of these twenty-six thirteen are in the non-subsidized middle-income housing group. About 18% of the low-income sample are saving for the future, as compared with 45% of the middle-income sample. Doubtless, this is a function of their higher incomes. Moreover, these low-middle-income women consider themselves to be working class. On a self-placement question 82% of these women placed themselves as lower class or working class, as compared with 74% of the low-income wives. Thus, the two subsamples are similar in terms of occupational level. However, the middle-income group is largely composed of the higher-status members of the working class. Their husbands' occupations are of somewhat higher status, although generally blue-collar; their incomes are higher and more stable, probably because more wives are working; their education is somewhat greater; and their orientation to the future seems more optimistic. In addition, they are residing in better housing than the low-income subsample, taken as a whole, since all of them live in a 221(d)3 project-type development designed for moderate-income families.

Some Comparisons. It is the intent of this chapter to examine variation in primary, secondary, and tertiary participation by status; this will be accomplished by comparing the low-income group with the middle-income group in the Boston sample.

What do we know about status differences in primary group interaction, such as friendship, neighboring, and kinship contact? The available data on status differences in the extent of friendship are almost exclusively based on whites and involve a variety of definitions of status. Hay found for a rural sample that friendship participation correlated positively with socioeconomic status: higher-status families congregated with friends more often.[5] This finding has been replicated by the Lynds in Middletown, by Williams for South Carolina housewives, by Axelrod for his urban Detroit sample, and by Bell and Boat for a San Francisco sample.[6] In all cases the higher status groups had somewhat more contact with friends or more friends on the average than lower status groups. Dotson's finding that 40% of his working-class families had no intimate friends (outside of relatives) fits well with these findings, as do the suggestions of Mogey, Berger, and Willmott that most of their working-class families had few social contacts outside of kin ties.[7] Only one study seems to contradict these findings. Reiss' careful time budget analysis revealed that high-status urban men had slightly less frienship contact, measured in terms of per diem minutes spent with "close intimate" and "good" friends, than did lower-status urban men.[8]

Few studies have carefully examined internal differences within the lower or working class. Axelrod's three lowest status levels, and the percentage of respondents at each level seeing friends (excluding co-workers) at least a few times a month, can be paralleled with the findings of Williams in South Carolina.[9] These data suggest that the positive correlation between socioeconomic status and friendship contact holds up to some extent even for the three lowest status levels in a set of six status levels. Unfortunately, no data seem to be available for black respondents. Yet it does seem plausible, on the basis of the general picture presented by these studies of whites, to posit the following: lower-income (or lower-blue-collar) blacks will have less contact with friends than middle-income (or upper-blue-collar) blacks.

The tabulations in Table 7:2 suggest that this is the case for the Roxbury area sample. Over six-tenths of the middle-income respondents had a high level of contact with friends as compared with one-quarter of the low-income respondents. Only 14% of the middle-income wives fall into the lowest level of friendship contact, while 37% of the low-income respondents are quite low in terms of friendship interaction. In addition, the amount of phone contact with friends and the extent of friend help in moving correlates positively with economic status. Thus, integration into city life by means of friendship is, to some degree, more substantial for the somewhat higher-status respondents in the Boston sample. Friends are seen somewhat more often, called somewhat more often, and depended upon for help a bit more often.

TABLE 7:2

FRIENDSHIP CONTACT BY STATUS
BOSTON SAMPLE (N=120)

Contact With Friends	Low-Income Group		Middle-Income Group		Total	
	Percent	N	Percent	N	Percent	N
Low	37.4%	(34)	13.8%	(4)	31.7%	(38)
Medium	37.4%	(34)	24.1	(7)	34.2%	(41)
High	25.3%	(23)	62.1	(18)	34.2%	(41)
Total	100.1%	(91)	100.0%	(29)	100.1%	(120)

$x^2 = 13.40.$ p $<.01.$

Since friendship interaction has been found to go hand-in-hand with neighboring, one might well predict that the higher-status wives would neighbor the most. The hypothesis is warranted on the basis of some previous data. The aforementioned San Juan study, which included a number of non-white families, found that higher-status families were substantially more intimate with their neighbors than lower-status families.[10] Tilly found that white-collar respondents, native or recent migrants, neighbored more than blue-collar respondents.[11] Likewise, the research of Fava, Whyte, and Smith, Form and Stone also suggests that neighboring should be widespread for higher-status respondents.[12]

However, others have reported divergent findings. Cohen and Hodges report that the lower-lower-class subjects made more visits for borrowing and exchange to their neighbors than did members of the upper-lower class and the lower middle class.[13] In his Detroit study Axelrod found that the lowest status group neighbored more than some higher status groups, but substantially less than the status group just above it; and Bell and Boat found that respondents from a large-family, low-economic-status area actually got together with their neighbors significantly more often than did respondents from a large-family, high economic-status area.[14] Such conflicting findings suggest that neighboring is not a unified phenomenon. Cohen and Hodges' findings propose a possible explanation. They found that lower-status respondents made more visits to their neighbors for borrowing than did higher-status respondents, but fewer visits for "pure" socializing; that is, they did less entertaining and had fewer parties than did higher-status families.[1]

The data in Table 7:3 indicate that the higher-status Roxbury area respondents do neighbor somewhat more than the rest, although the relationship is not statistically significant.

TABLE 7:3

NEIGHBORING BY STATUS
BOSTON SAMPLE (N=119)[a]

Neighboring	Low-Income Group		Middle-Income Group		Total	
	Percent	N	Percent	N	Percent	N
Low	40.0%	(36)	31.0%	(9)	37.8%	(45)
Medium	27.8%	(25)	20.7	(6)	26.1%	(31)
High	32.2%	(29)	48.3	(14)	36.1%	(43)
Total	100.0%	(90)	100.0%	(29)	100.0%	(119)

$x^2 = 2.45$ n.s.

[a]An N in this table (or elsewhere) not equal to 120 indicates that respondents were omitted because of incomplete answers to the question(s) at issue.

About 48% of the low-middle-income group had a high level of neighboring as compared with one-third of the low-income group. Correspondingly, 31% of the low-middle-income group and 40% of the low-income group fell in the lowest third of neighboring scale scores. To some extent these findings suggest that -- even for ghetto residents -- neighboring is more extensive for the higher-status members of the blue-collar class. It should be kept in mind that all of the low-middle-income sample are now living in 221(d)3 housing, a physical setting which may encourage neighboring. Only about two-thirds of the low-income families are currently residing in a comparable project or quasi-project milieu.

A third type of primary integration into urban social life is through kinship networks. The evidence on status differences in kin contact is conflicting. Several studies have found greater contact for blue-collar, versus white-collar, respondents. Blue-collar respondents in Wilmington, Delware reported more contiguous kin and more frequent kin contact than white-collar respondents.[16] Moreover, blue-collar respondents were more likely to have migrated exclusively under the auspices of kin than white-collar respondents.[17] Certainly one gets an impression of a kin-dominated working class society in the various case studies, including those of Willmott, Young, Mogey and Berger.[18] In addition to Tilly's study, cited above, the detailed findings of Reiss give some support to such status differences in kin contact.[19] A caution is, however, in order. Litwak's several articles have demonstrated that the extended family is still important even for the more mobile members of the middle class.[20] In one study he reports that extended family orientation increases as one moves up the status scale, although he does not have evidence indicating a concomitant increase in kin contact. Other researchers have found kin contact to be quite similar at almost all status levels. Axelrod found that, except for one of his middle classes which was somewhat more kin-oriented, about 60% of each status level associated with relatives at least a few times a month.[21] Based on a survey of social areas in San Francisco, Bell and Boat found that the intensity of interaction with relatives was roughly the same for respondents in a high familism, low economic area and in a high familism, high economic area.[22] For these several white samples the data indicate no consistent pattern; and no data appear to be available on black families.

What was the finding for the sample of black Bostonians. Table 7:4 presents the evidence. A somewhat greater proportion of the low-middle-income group than of the low-income group fall at the highest level of kin contact. About 41% of the higher-status housewives had a high intensity of kin contact, while 31% of the lower-status group had a high level of contact. Approximately 24% of the higher-status respondents fell into the lower third of intensity scores; 15% more of the lower-status respondents fell into this lower level of kin contact. It can be seen, however, that the relationship between status and kin contact is rather weak. An overall impression of differences between the higher-status group and the lower-status group is gained from looking at the three types of primary interaction. In all three primary areas the higher-status group seems to be a little more active in the social life of the black ghetto community. Especially in the area of friendship do they appear to have an advantage. In the case of kinship and neighboring the postive relationship between status and contact is rather weak. Yet this conclusion should not be misconstrued, for most of the low-income respondents _fell_ _at_ _moderate_ _to_ _high_ _levels_ _of_ _social_ _interaction_.

TABLE 7:4

KINSHIP CONTACT BY STATUS
BOSTON SAMPLE (N=120)

Kin Contact	Low-Income Group		Middle-Income Group		Total	
	Percent	N	Percent	N	Percent	N
Low	39.6%	(36)	24.1%	(7)	35.8%	(43)
Medium	29.7%	(27)	34.5%	(10)	30.8%	(37)
High	30.8%	(28)	41.4%	(12)	33.3%	(40)
Total	100.1%	(91)	100.0%	(29)	99.9%	(120)

χ^2=2.37. n.s.

Does this advantage for the low-middle-income respondents extend to the sphere of secondary associations? In an analysis of the NORC poll data for urban areas Hausknecht found that voluntary association membership varied directly with socioeconomic indices.[23] Using three major status variables, income, occupation, and education, he found that the better paid and better educated respondents tended to belong to more secondary organizations than their less well-off counterparts. Professionals and skilled workers belonged to more organizations than semi-skilled and unskilled workers.

Many other researchers, such as Zimmer, Axelrod, Chapin, Hay, Scott, and Tilly have also discovered a positive correlation between association membership and socioeconomic status.[24] Focussing specifically on a blue-collar sample, Cohen and Hodges found a substantial difference in associational participation (including churches and unions) between a lower-blue-collar group and an upper-blue-collar group, the latter being far more associationally integrated than the former.[25] They argue that the lower status group lacks the skills and resources for extensive associational activity. The data analyzed by Hamilton reveal a similar difference in associational participation between the higher and lower status members of the blue-collar class.[26] Although he discovered a differential in favor of the upper-blue-collar class, he found that this sub-class was closer to the lower-blue-collar class in association participation than to a white-collar comparison group.

Again, little systematic information is available for black communities. A study of a Lincoln, Nebraska community found that home-owning blacks participate more actively in secondary associations than those who are renters; other status variations were not explored.[27] One does get the impression from certain case studies, such as Black Metropolis and Blackways of Kent, that higher-status families are more active in secondary associations than lower-status ones.[28] However, this impression is fogged by the accompanying reports of extensive religious participation, albeit sect participation, of the lower classes.

The Boston data seem to confirm, to some extent, the previous findings on whites, as well as the data of Babchuk, Drake, and Lewis on black respondents (Table 7:5). About 48% of the higher status group had a high level of organizational participation; about one-quarter of the lower status group had a correspondingly high level of association. Likewise, the lower-income group had a substantially greater percentage (37.4%) than the higher-income group falling at the lowest participation level. Even for this black sample it seems clear that the economically better-off respondents tend to be better integrated into the local urban subcommunity through secondary or associational ties than their low-income counterparts. Cohen and Hodges' explanation of this differentiation seems plausible for this Boston sample. They argue that people join organizations (1) because they have a stake in its goals and (2) because of social relationships.[29] Since the goals of most community and city-wide organizations are oriented to the status levels above the poverty line, it is reasonable to expect low-income respondents to avoid such organizations, with the exception of churches. It is also important to consider the possibility that the low-middle-income respondents may have more time for such pursuits.

TABLE 7:5

ORGANIZATIONAL PARTICIPATION BY STATUS
BOSTON SAMPLE (N=120)

Organizational Participation	Low-Income Group		Middle-Income Group		Total	
	Percent	N	Percent	N	Percent	N
Low	37.4%	(34)	20.7%	(6)	33.3%	(40)
High	36.3	(33)	31.0	(9)	35.0	(42)
Medium	26.4	(24)	48.3	(14)	31.7	(38)
Total	100.1%	(91)	100.0%	(29)	100.0%	(120)

$x^2 = 5.34$. p $<.10$.

Should one also expect status differences in the area of tertiary participation? The lack of previous data makes predictions difficult. Using the measure of activities described in an earlier chapter, Roxbury area interviewers quizzed each respondent on the frequency of her trips into the local community as well as into downtown and the greater Boston area. It should be remembered that 80% to 90% of the whole sample had never done any of the activities listed except "going riding around in the car for pleasure" and "gone downtown to a movie." The two status groups are quite similar on all activities except for going downtown to a movie and for attendance at a civil rights meeting. Although only 24% of the total sample, the middle-income respondents were about 37% of those who had gone downtown to a movie or to a civil rights meeting in the last two months. Their likelihood of venturing out to a downtown movie is greater probably because they are more likely to have the requisite financial resources. This figure on movie-going and civil rights meeting attendance jibes with the small difference in favor of the higher status group found in regard to associational activity. Comparisons of the two groups on the number of and destination of shopping, business, and medical trips, revealed no surprises. Comparing the percent who made no trips, the percentage differences were 10% or less in all cases, favoring the low-income group in regard to shopping trips. With regard to the geographical range of shopping the two groups are similar in their dependence on the ghetto area.

Newspaper reading has been found to vary directly with status measured in terms of education. Bogart reports several studies which indicate that newspaper reading is greatest for those with a college education and goes down as education decreases: 53% of grade school graduates were found to read a newspaper daily as compared with 65% of high school graduates and 77% of college graduates.[30] An occupational breakdown did not turn up any significant

differences between semi-skilled, skilled, or professional workers in the
extent of newspaper readership; the unskilled were only a little less likely
to read a newspaper on an average weekday.

TABLE 7:6

BOSTON PAPER READERSHIP BY STATUS
BOSTON SAMPLE (N=119)

Frequency of Newspaper Reading	Low-Income Group		Middle-Income Group		Total	
	Percent	N	Percent	N	Percent	N
Less than daily	37.8%	(34)	27.6%	(8)	35.3%	(42)
Daily	62.2	(56)	72.4	(21)	64.7	(77)
Total	100.0%	(90)	100.0%	(29)	100.0%	(119)

$x^2 = .998$. n.s.

The data for the Boston sample reveal that the middle-income respondents are
a bit more likely to read a metropolitan paper daily than their lower-income
counterparts, although the overwhelming majority of both groups are daily
readers. About 72% of the higher status group and 62% of the lower status
group read one of the Boston papers daily. This agrees with the minor
difference in readership which Bogart reports. With regard to local community
newspapers Janowitz reported that 84% of his Chicago respondents were readers
of their local paper.[31] Bogart reports a study showing that grade and high
school graduates are much more interested in city news than in international
news as contrasted with the more internationalist minded college graduates.[32]
Consideration of this finding and the fact that the Roxbury area respondents
have a mean level of education of 10.3 to 11.1 suggests that both status
groups, if blacks parallel whites, should have a large number of local newspaper fans. The findings tabulated in Table 7:7 do not support this expectation. The majority of both subsamples do not regularly read either of the local
papers. The differences between the two socioeconomic groups are not striking;
and they actually would offer a little support to the hypothesis that middle-
income families are more interested in local news than their low-income
counterparts.

As noted in an earlier chapter, the importantce of television viewing
and radio listening for Americans -- at least white Americans -- has been
documented in several studies. With regard to status differences in mass
media contact Bogart reports data indicating that operatives and laborers

tend to report higher levels of exposure to television than other occupational groups.[33] Clarke and Komarovsky report that lower-status (or blue-collar) respondents prefer TV watching to other forms of leisure.[34] In the afore-mentioned study of Boston whites, Sweetser found that his white-collar respondents spent an average of 2.16 hours a weekday watching TV and his blue-collar respondents had a weekday average of 2.52 hours.[35]

TABLE 7:7

ROXBURY PAPER READERSHIP BY STATUS
BOSTON SAMPLE (N=119)

Frequency of Newspaper Reading	Low-Income Group		Middle-Income Group		Total	
	Percent	N	Percent	N	Percent	N
Not at all	40.0%	(36)	34.5%	(10)	38.7%	(46)
Occasionally	35.6	(32)	34.5	(10)	35.3	(42)
Weekly	24.4	(22)	31.0	(9)	26.0	(31)
Total	100.0%	(90)	100.0%	(29)	100.0%	(119)

x^2 = .546. n.s.

These findings certainly suggest that a blue-collar sample would spend more time before the television set than white-collar families. However, only one study seems to have examined internal variations within the lower -- and working -- classes. Using the ISC index, White found that females in the upper-lower class spent somewhat more time watching television than lower-lower-class females.[36] The following hypothesis would follow from this: the higher-status blue-collar group in the general Roxbury area sample should be more oriented to the TV than their lower-status counterparts. For the type of status division used in analyzing the Roxbury area findings there is no support for this hypothesis (Table 7:8).

TABLE 7:8

TV WATCHING BY STATUS
BOSTON SAMPLE (N=120)

Time Spent Watching TV	Low-Income Group		Middle-Income Group		Total	
	Percent	N	Percent	N	Percent	N
Low (0-1¼ hours)	33.0%	(30)	34.5%	(10)	33.3%	(40)
Medium (1½-3¼ hours)	29.7	(27)	27.6	(8)	29.2	(35)
High (3½ hours or more)	37.4	(34)	37.9	(11)	37.5	(45)
Total	100.1%	(91)	100.0%	(29)	100.0%	(120)

$x^2 = .05.$ n.s.

The distributions for the two income groups are virtually identical.

When the amount of time allocated in the time budget question to all types of mass media contact (TV, radio, newspaper, magazines) is computed, small differences between the two groups do appear. Table 7:9 indicates that low-income respondents are more likely than middle-income respondents to maintain a high level of media contact. About 36% of the low-income group sustained a high level of contact with the radio and TV, while less than a quarter of the middle-income wives reported contact of a comparable level. However, the middle-income wives also had the smallest percentage in the low-contact third. The obvious reason for this is that nearly half of them fell into the middle range, from two and one-quarter hours to four and one-half hours of TV and radio contact. The overall differences appear to be accounted for by the greater amount of radio listening of the lower-blue-collar housewives.

Page Number98

TABLE 7:9

MASS MEDIA CONTACT BY STATUS
BOSTON SAMPLE (N=120)

Mass Media Contact	Low-Income Group		Middle-Income Group		Total	
	Percent	N	Percent	N	Percent	N
Low (0-2 hours)	34.1	(31)	27.6%	(8)	32.5%	(39)
Medium ($2\frac{1}{4}$-$4\frac{1}{2}$ hours)	29.7	(27)	48.3	(14)	34.2	(41)
High (4-$15\frac{1}{4}$ hours)	36.3	(33)	24.1	(7)	33.3	(40)
Total	100.1%	(91)	100.0%	(29)	100.0%	(120)

x^2 = 3.48. n.s.

Conclusion

The status differential between the low-income group, composed of families in public, private, and 221(d)3 housing, and the low-middle-income group, composed only of families in 221(d)3 housing, seems to be primarily one of income. Each of the subsamples is predominantly blue-collar, both in terms of husbands' occupation and subjective class placement.

Participation differences have previously been found between lower-blue-collar respondents and upper-blue-collar respondents, usually favoring the latter. On the whole, the data on the Boston sample suggest, paralleling most of these studies, that upper-blue-collar respondents are somewhat better integrated into the urban social fabric than the lower-blue-collar respondents. A summary of the data indicating the direction of difference substantiates this point. However, it should be noted that only one of the chi-squares for the differentials was significant at the .05 level. In the area of primary contacts the low- middle-income groups is, to some degree, better integrated than the low-income subjects, whether the comparison be neighboring, friendship contact, or kin contact. Likewise they are better integrated in terms of the extent of their participation in voluntary associations. Even in the area of tertiary participation the middle-income group has somewhat greater contact with the metropolitan and local newspapers, and about the same degree of contact with the TV.

However, the differences are not very great; and the low-income group did make a few more trips into the city and have somewhat greater contact

with all the mass media taken together than did the middle-income respondents.
Thus one must not press these small differentials very hard. More evidence
is needed. Thus Table 7:10 gives some confirmation of the expectations,
suggested by previous studies, of status differences in social participation.
Additional variation in participation will be examined in the next chapter;
there the focus will be on the effects of a short-range move.

TABLE 7:10

SUMMARY OF DATA TABLES
BOSTON SAMPLE (N=120)

Direction of Difference	Number of Times		
	Primary Contact	Secondary Contact	Tertiary Contact
Middle-income group Somewhat better integrated than low-income group	3	1	2
Low-income group Somewhat better integrated than middle-income group	0	0	1
Neither better integrated than the other	0	0	1

FOOTNOTES

(Chapter 7)

[1]Section 221(d)3 of the 1961 Housing Act provides for below-market FHA financing for organizations which will build new housing in urban renewal areas. "221(d)3 housing" in the text refers to such (quasi-project) housing built in the Roxbury urban renewal area.

[2]Robert J. Lampman, The Low Income Population and Economic Growth (Joint Economic Committee of Congress, Study Paper, No. 12; Washington: Government Printing Office, 1959).

[3]Conference on Economic Progress, Poverty and Deprivation in the United States (Washington, 1961). Cited in S. M. Miller, "The 'New' Working Class," Blue-Collar World, eds. Arthur B. Shostak and William Gomberg (Englewood Cliffs, New Jersey: Prentice-Hall, 1964), p.3. This report is sometimes called the "Keyserling report."

[4]This average of $5,300 for these relatively large families is sub-stantially less than the current national average (1964: $6,570). Considering this and the fact that these are predominantly blue-collar families, it might be more appropriate to term these families "upper-blue-collar" or "stable-working-class" rather than "middle-income." In any case, "middle-income," a term used by the builders of their 221(d)3 housing, should not necessarily be taken to mean "middle-class."

[5]Hay, op. cit., pp. 285ff.

[6]Lynd and Lynd, op. cit., pp. 272ff.; Axelrod, op. cit., p. 728; Bell and Boat, op. cit., p. 394; and James H. Williams, "Close Friendship Relations of Housewives Residing in an Urban Community," Social Forces, 36 (1958), 358-362.

[7]Dotson, op. cit., p. 691; Berger, op. cit., pp. 55ff.; Mogey, op. cit., p. 96 and passim; Young and Willmott, op. cit., passim.

[8]Albert J. Reiss, Jr., "Rural-Urban and Status Differences in Interpersonal Contacts," American Journal of Sociology, 65 (1959), 188.

[9] Axelrod, op. cit., p.728; Williams, op. cit., p.359.

[10]Caplow, Stryker, and Wallace, op. cit., pp. 162-163.

[11] Tilly, Migration to an American City, loc. cit., p. 34.

[12]William H. Whyte, Jr., op. cit.; Smith, Form and Stone, op. cit.; and Fava, op. cit.

[13]Cohen and Hodges, op. cit., pp.313ff.

[14]Axelrod, op. cit., p. 728; and Bell and Boat, op. cit., p.394.

[15]Cohen and Hodges, op. cit., p. 314.

[16]Tilly, Migration to an American City, loc. cit., p. 35.

[17]Tilly and Brown, op. cit., pp. 17-18.

[18]Young and Willmott, op. cit.; Mogey, op. cit.; Berger, op. cit. However, Blum, takes issue with this view and presents a little evidence to the contrary. Alan F. Blum, "Social Structure, Social Class, and Participation in Primary Relationships," Blue-Collar World, eds. Arthur B. Shostak and William Gomberg (Englewood Cliffs, New Jersey: Prentice-Hall, 1964), pp. 203-204.

[19] Reiss, op. cit., pp. 188ff.

[20]Litwak, op. cit., p. 17.

[21]Axelrod, op. cit., p.728.

[22]Bell and Boat, op. cit., p. 394.

[23]Hausknecht, op. cit., pp. 27-30.

[24]Basil G. Zimmer, "Participation of Migrants in Urban Structures," Cities and Society, eds. Paul K. Hatt and Albert J. Reiss, Jr. (New York: The Free Press of Glencoe, 1957), pp. 732-733; Axelrod, op. cit., p.725; Chapin, op. cit., p. 160; Hay, op. cit., p. 291; Scott, op. cit., p. 321; and Tilly, Migration to an American City, loc. cit., p. 33. Cf. also Blum, op. cit., p. 202.

[25]Cohen and Hodges, op. cit., p. 315.

[26]Richard Hamilton, "The Behavior and Values of Skilled Workers," Blue-Collar World, eds. Arthur Shostak and William Gomberg (Englewood Cliffs, New Jersey: Prentice-Hall, 1964), p. 48.

[27]Babchuk and Thompson, op. cit., p. 652.

[28] For example, Drake and Cayton, op. cit., p. 669; and Lewis, op. cit., pp. 256-267.

[29]Cohen and Hodges, op. cit., p. 315.

[30]Bogart, op. cit., p. 425.

[31]Janowitz, op. cit., p. 208.

[32]Bogart, op. cit., p.425.

[33]Ibid., p. 420. Cf. also Steiner, op. cit.

102

[34]Alfred C. Clarke, "The Use of Leisure and Its Relation to Levels of Occupational Prestige," American Sociological Review, 21 (1956), 304; and Komarovsky, Blue-Collar Marriage, loc. cit., p. 324.

[35]Sweetser, op. cit., p. 82.

[36]R. Clyde White, "Social Class Differences in the Uses of Leisure," Mass Leisure, eds. Eric Larrabee and Rolf Meyersohn (Glencoe, Illinois: Free Press, 1958), p. 202.

MOBILITY AND SOCIAL PARTICIPATION

Short-range geographical mobility has generally been neglected by students of migration; the predominant concern has been with inter-country or rural-urban migration. In addition, few studies dealing with intra-urban mobility have been longitudinal, examining the effects of a move with "before" and "after" interviews. Housing researchers have conducted longitudinal investigations of intra-urban moves, but even they have not examined the effect of the move per se, as distinguished from the effect of the housing environment.

What is the general view of the effects of intra-city migration on the social ties of urban families? Two basic questions seem to be suggested by available data: one view is that geographical mobility is essentially a process characterized by social disorder and disorganization, severance of important interpersonal ties, and grief. This has been the view presented by several studies done in Lagos, Nigeria, Oxford, England, and London, England. The net effect of changing neighborhoods was a general decline in inter-personal contacts. Marris' study of housing estate families who moved out of central Lagos revealed a low degree of contact with relatives compared to families still in the central area.[1] Willmott and Young investigated a housing estate in East London and found a similar phenomenon in regard not only to relatives but also to other social contacts.[2] Mogey's data on Oxford (England) housing estate families also support this same argument for the disruptive effects of neighborhood change, at least in regard to the severance of ties with relatives.[3] But he did find more extensive friendship activity in the estate than in his comparable central city sample. Some published data are also available on American respondents. Fried's study of Italian-Americans displaced by urban renewal from Boston's West End revealed that many were overcome with grief as a result of the disruptive effects of a move out of an area characterized by intimate social ties.[4] Fried implies that such an involuntary move meant, for the average respondent, a net loss of inter-personal interaction, at least in the short run.

By contrast, mobility has been seen by others as basically an orderly process in which centripetal social forces predominate. For example, residential mobility is viewed by Gans, at least the voluntary move of an middle-class family, as an orderly process foreseen and specifically chosen by the family.[5] Gans argues that middle-class movers to suburbs are usually looking for and generally find increased sociability. Thus, changing neighborhoods is not only not disruptive but often means a net gain in interpersonal contacts. Similarly, research on public housing (working-class) families in Baltimore and Minneapolis found that a move from a deteriorated neighborhood to a better quality housing environment stimulated an increase in sociability as measured by questions on neighboring patterns and associational ties.[6]

None of the aforementioned studies differentiates between the short-term
and the long-term effects of short-range residential mobility. It may be
that the disruptive effects of intra-urban mobility are initial and that
most families reestablish social ties in a relatively short time in the
new environment. If they move into a substantially improved socio-physical
environment they may even surpass their previous level of social interaction.
The basic model might be as follows: Mobility is a two-step process which
involves traversing physical distance and breaking or temporarily severing
current social ties. The short-term impact of the move may be to sever (or
at least to stretch) established social ties. Depending on the type of
tie and the distance moved, the first few weeks after the move will generally
show a net decrease in social interaction. In the same first few weeks new
social ties also begin to form, and the long-term effect of the new housing
environment is either a regaining of the previous level of social interaction
or a net increase in social interaction if the new housing environment is
one which promotes interaction. Such a model combines insights from the
two general views of mobility and partially reduces the apparent conflict
between them.

The Boston Samples

In earlier chapters I have focussed upon the social participation patterns
of the sample of black Bostonians, paralleling their profile with that of
other samples on which comparable research has been done. An original
purpose of study was an interest in the effects which geographical mobility
would have upon these links into urban social life. As noted in Chapter II,
the overall Roxbury area sample actually includes four groups of movers,
families who moved generally within the ghetto area of Boston. Although
the original matched set design had to be given up, the four samples are
roughly matched in regard to race, age of wife, number of children, family
type, and income (except for the low-middle-income group). The initial pools
were not large enough to pick thirty-five matched sets of four; and some of
those originally in the successfully matched sets did not move. These factors
affect the overall matching, although the samples are still roughly similar
as can be seen in Table 8:1. There are three significant differences which
should be noted. Although all four samples are composed of large families,
the rent supplementation sample has the largest mean number of children;
and the public housing sample is different in two respects. It has fewer
male-headed families and a lower mean income. Of course, the middle-
income sample does have the highest mean income, as expected. All of
these families were administered an "after-move" questionnaire which included a broad range of social participation questions; but the "before-
move" interview included fewer participation items. However, at least one
index in each of the general areas of primary, secondary, and tertiary
participation is available from both interviews and will be used in the
following analysis.

Before looking at the data on social participation, it is necessary
to examine three preliminary questions which bear upon the social integration of families on the move: (1) How far were the moves? (2) Were
the moves involuntary? (3) Is the new housing environment really an
improved one?

TABLE 8:1

DESCRIPTIVE STATISTICS ON FOUR MOBILITY SAMPLES
(N=104)

	Number	Age of Wife (Mean)	Number of Children (Mean)	Income (Mean)	Percentage Male-headed Families
Private housing sample	16	32	3.9	$4500	50%
Public housing sample	24	30	3.8	$3100	38%
Rent supplementation sample	35	30	5.6	$4100	59%
Middle-income sample	29	33	4.7	$5300	60%

How far were the moves? Table 8:2 indicates the distances moved by respondents in each of the four Roxbury area housing samples. On the average, the rent supplementation sample, all of whom were forced to move because of urban renewal, moved the shortest distance: approximately six city blocks.

TABLE 8:2

MEAN DISTANCE MOVED
BOSTON SAMPLES

	Number	Mean (in Miles)
Rent supplementation sample	35	.57
Middle-income sample	29	.86
Public housing sample	24	2.05
Private housing sample	16	1.01
All samples	104	1.01

The low-middle-income sample moved about nine city blocks on the average, while the private housing group averaged approximately one mile. The public housing group traversed the greatest distance by far of all the housing groups: a mean of about two miles. Thus, on the average, these Roxbury area respondents

moved only a moderate distance away from their old neighborhoods. Such a
distance is substantially shorter than that travelled by the housing estate
respondents in the British and African studies, some of which found the move
disruptive for their kinship ties.[8] It probably approximates the relatively
shorter distances moved by the low-income families whom Wilner and Chapin
studied; these two studies found an increase in social participation with
a move into an improved housing environment.[9] The relatively moderate
distances travelled by the Boston movers would incline one to accept the order
view of geographical mobility for predictive purposes.

Table 8:3 reports information obtained from the respondents in reply to
questions concerning why they had moved; in cases where direct replies were
inadequate, data from other questions bearing on housing experiences or from
housing agency records were used to fill in the gaps. All of the subsidy
tenants, most of the private tenants, and a majority of the middle-income sample
were more or less forced to move, either by the Boston Redevelopment Authority's
site clearance procedures or by deteriorating housing often on the fringe of
renewal areas. Only 38% of the public sample were forced to move in this sense.
These data emphasize the difference between these black samples and certain other
white (and usually white-collar) samples which have been studied.

TABLE 8:3

REASONS FOR MOBILITY

		Reasons			
	Number	Because of Urban Renewal	Because of Deteriorated Housing	Other	Total
Rent supplementation sample	35	100%	0	0	100%
Middle-income sample	29	28%	31	41	100%
Public housing sample	24	17%	21	62	100%
Private housing sample	16	75%	12	13	100%

For such a sample, Rossi argues that the life cycle is the important generator
of housing complaints, mobility desires, and actual mobility. Under pressure
from a growing family, young families move toward increased space and a house
of their own. When space is no longer needed, older couples tend to move away
from such residences.[10] Gans has noted that certain (white) middle-class
families voluntarily move out to suburbs for the additional purpose of
increasing their social interaction;[11] this selectivity phenomenon, he avers,
partially accounts for the higher degree of sociability in the suburbs.

However, most of the Boston sample can under no circumstances be considered voluntary movers seeking to follow the family cycle or to satisfy their longings for increased sociability. About 57% were forced to move by urban renewal and an additional 15% because of deteriorated or dilapidated housing. Thus, at least 72% were forced to enter the housing market whether or not they actually wanted to do so; the comparable figure for mobile families in general is 2% to 3%. Selectivity may still have played a part in whether they chose to apply to a project or to move again in the private housing market. But the supply of proximate private housing had been substantially decreased by discrimination and by urban renewal, and many of the families undoubtedly had no choice but to apply to public housing, or, if they could afford it, to the 221(d)3 projects. Thus, selectivity -- in the sense of a person choosing a project solely in order to increase social interaction -- does not seem to be an important factor in the housing choices of most of these Negro families.

TABLE 8:4

HOUSING IMPROVEMENT (BUILDING CONDITION)[a]
BOSTON SAMPLE

	Number	Mean Before	Mean After	Net Change
Rent supplementation sample	35	1.54	4.57	+3.03
Middle-income sample	29	1.85	4.65	+2.70
Public housing sample	24	1.25	3.17	+1.92
Private housing sample	16	1.31	2.37	+1.06

[a]Respondents' housing structures were classified by the interviewers into five ranked categories from +1=very poor housing (three or more basic structural items needing repair) to +5=excellent (high quality construction, well cared for). Note that the "mean before" for all groups is very low, indicating that the bulk of the respondents lived in deteriorating housing before the move.

Table 8:4 indicates the significant housing improvement which the three project groups experienced and the slight improvement which the private housing group experienced. The amelioration is most substantial in regard to the rent supplementation group, followed in order by the middle-income, public housing, and private housing groups. The improvement of the private housing group is not as significant as the others; it should be noted that they are still residing in housing which is somewhat dilapidated, needing one or two structural repairs on the average. The aforementioned studies of families moving out of dilapidated slum housing -- those studies lending weight to the non-disruptive model of mobility -- argue strongly for the positive effects that a substantially meliorated housing environment can have upon the social lives of families. Following their line of argument, one would predict that the Boston families, especially those in the three project groups, should become increasingly enmeshed in intimate social ties as a result of a change in housing from slum residences to better quality housing.

Social Participation Variables

Because of the difficulties mentioned in Chapter II the Boston respondents were interviewed at varying intervals after their moves from one neighborhood to another. As a result "after-move" interviews were completed from one week to one year after the move. This, of course, poses a problem in any direct comparisons of the several housing groups. However, this difficulty can be made a virtue; within each of the housing groups respondents have been in their new housing environments for varying lengths of time. A change score ("after" score less the "before" score) was computed for each of these respondents. The figures on subsequent pages plot mean change scores for each of the several housing groups at four different points in time after the move-in. This was done to get around the problem of selectivity involved in the arbitrary dividing of each housing group into four subdivisions.

These figures were set up as follows: The three samples of project movers were combined, and the combined group was divided into approximate quartiles according to the number of weeks which had elapsed between the date of "move-in" and the date of the follow-up interview. Then the members of each of the three project samples which fell within each quartile were treated as a distinct group for the purposes of the graphs. Fortunately the several project samples were crudely matched for date of move. Each time point has, on the average, a quarter of each of the subsamples within its limits, although the range is from 17% to 33%. There are several points which should be kept in mind when reflecting on the graphs. The number of respondents in each of the "time-in" groups is rather small, ranging from five to twelve depending on the size of that particular subsample. Because of the difficulty of selecting a control group of private movers, the matching on "time-in" was generally not possible; the total group of private movers available was only sixteen. This group could not, therefore, be divided into groups comparable to those for the project samples; the private sample was split into two subgroups, approximately at the median time elapsed since the move. These two groups (two time points) are plotted on the graphs for comparison purposes. On the whole, this procedure seemed to be the only way to differentiate, however tentatively, between the effects of the move itself and the socio-physical housing environment. At best this kind of analysis is suggestive, and the graphs should be interpreted with caution. Yet they are inherently interesting.

Thus, the change scores represent net increases and decreases in social participation. What the figures present, beyond the (longitudinal) before-after time comparison involved in the change scores themselves, is a diachronic simulation using cross-sectional data. Preceding each of the figures will be a brief table indicating the absolute mean scores on each of the housing samples before and after the move.

The first type of primary participation to be examined will be neighboring. On the basis of previous research what did we expect? The findings of a longitudinal study of Baltimore respondents moving into public housing units suggested the forecast that the Roxbury area respondents moving into project housing would gain in neighboring.[1] However, the gain for the black families in Baltimore was measured at the end of a <u>three-year period</u>; no evidence was presented on the short-run effect of the move <u>per se</u>. What were the Boston findings?

Before looking at the neighborhood curves in Figure 8:1 it is worth examining the absolute mean scores in Table 8:5. Simple comparisons of "before" and "after" means (or percentages) is the usual analytical procedure in the few extant longitudinal studies of housing and mobility.

TABLE 8:5

MEAN NEIGHBORING SCORES

	Rent Supplementation Sample		Middle-Income Sample		Public Housing Sample		Private Housing Sample	
	Score	N	Score	N	Score	N	Score	N
"Before" mean	7.0	(35)	7.9	(28)	7.6	(23)	7.4	(15)
"After" mean	6.9	(35)	7.6	(29)	6.1	(24)	5.8	(15)

Using this type of comparison, inspection of the data in Table 8:5 reveals a decrease in mean neighboring scores with the move for each of the sub-samples. However, this simple comparison may well be hiding a decrease with the move and an increase with "time-in," as would be predicted on the basis of the model suggested earlier. For this reason the neighboring curve over time must be examined.[12]

Plotting the neighboring curves for the three project samples and the smaller sample of private movers reveals the most consistent phenomenon in all of the figures for the social participation variables (Figure 8:1). For each of the samples we find a sharp drop-off in neighboring during the first one to three weeks of residence. Neighboring, of the several types of social participation examined in this chapter, seems to be the most closely tied to, and affected by, the locality. Obviously one's relations with neighbors, <u>qua</u> neighbors, in the sending neighborhood are usually severed even by a rather short-range move. The data in figure 8:1 strongly support this interpretation.[13] Respondents in all four of the housing groups experienced a net loss in neighboring as a consequence of shifting from one locale to another. After all, neighbors in the new neighborhood generally are social strangers; and there seems to be some reticence on the part of recent migrants toward neighboring in a new environment during the first few weeks, the "settling-in" period. In fact, several of the Boston houswives expressed a desire to put their house in order before they did much neighboring.

NEIGHBORING: CHANGE SCORES FOR FOUR BOSTON SAMPLES

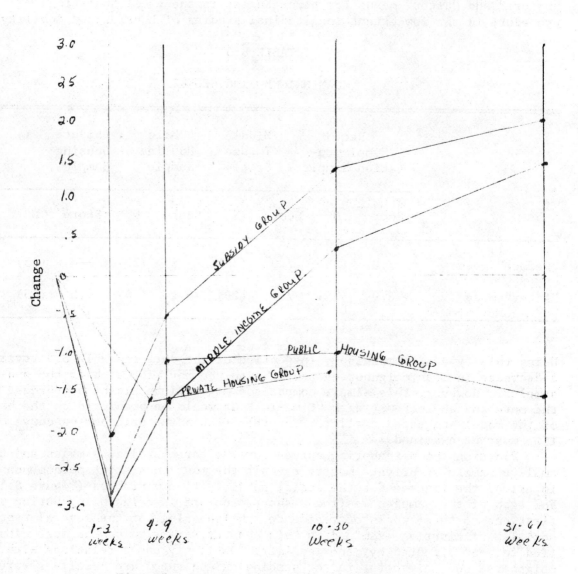

Time Elapsed Since Date of Move-in

Fig. 8:1.

Gradually, however, proximity comes into play, and chats occur between neighbors. As familiarity grows, the casual interaction graduates to reciprocal visiting and exchange of favors. This neighboring phenomenon eventually, for the 221(d)3 residents at later points in time, increases significantly beyond the level sustained in the sending neighborhoods. It should be noted that there is a real difficulty in differentiating the effect of the physical environment (space, proximity, etc.) and the effect of the social environment. In the case of these samples the new housing environment combines social and physical aspects which tend to defy attempts to separate them. A combination of such social and spatial factors may help to account for the net increase in neighboring for 221(d)3 families:

1. The relative homogeneity of the tenant population;
2. The greater probability of contact with residents in projects of relatively high density and/or of an architecture (courts, etc.) which fosters neighboring;
3. The increase in space and facilities for entertaining;
4. The common experience of adjusting to quite a new and substantially improved housing environment.

All of these bear in one way or another upon the impact which the socio-physical locale has upon the social lives of urban families and their neighboring patterns.

The public housing and private housing movers, by contrast, also experienced an initial decrease in neighboring just after the move. However, with time their level of neighboring, although rising above the nadir, does not at any point come up to their original level of neighboring. The initial drop-off in neighboring for the private movers is explicable in terms of the locale-based character of neighboring. The failure of the curve to rise as rapidly as that of the 221(d)3 families may be due to the absence of some of the social and/or spatial factors noted above. Certainly they did not experience as radical an improvement in housing as the 221(d)3 groups.

In any event, the last time point includes families who have been in their new residences at most forty weeks. With additional time their level of neighboring may approximate or even exceed the "before-move" level. The movement of the curve for the public housing families, beyond the initial decrease, is unexpected. It directly contradicts the findings of the Baltimore study. One possible ex post facto explanation for this may be in the fact that the public housing environment for many of these Boston respondents, although spatially somewhat of an improvement may be socially distressing and may foster distrust of some neighbors for some respondents. Plotting the change scores for a housing preference question (size, rent, schools, etc.) included in both the "before" and "after" interviews does reveal a gradual decrease in housing satisfaction, over time, for the public housing tenants as compared with a gradual increase in satisfaction for comparable respondents in the rent supplementation sample. In any case, the patterns for the two 221(d)3 groups at all stages and the pattern of the private and public housing groups in the first nine weeks support the contention that neighboring is the social participation phenomenon most affected by the very move itself, the change of locale, as distinguished from the particular type of housing environment; and the movement of the curves for the two 221(d)3 samples from the tenth week onward lends support to the argument that substantial improvements in the socio-physical environment can accelerate neighboring.

The effect of intra-city mobility on friendship contacts has not been systematically investigated. Mogey's data do indicate that former central city residents now residing out in housing projects ("housing estates") have more contact with friends than comparable families still residing in the central city.[14] In a study of working-class families Berger found a small increase in friendship interaction with the move to a suburb.[15] These studies indicate that the order model of mobility holds true over time and in improved housing environments in regard to friendship ties; but they offer no suggestions for the short-term effects of the move. However, it was expected for moves of a moderate distance, such as the one mile averaged by the Roxbury area respondents, that friendship interaction would not be affected as systematically as ties with neighbors were.

Table 8:6 presents the mean absolute scores for friendship contact before and after the move.

TABLE 8:6

MEAN CONTACT WITH FRIENDS

	Rent Supplementation Sample		Middle-Income Sample		Public Housing Sample		Private Housing Sample	
	Score	N	Score	N	Score	N	Score	N
"Before" mean	8.1	(35)	12.0	(29)	12.1	(24)	9.6	(16)
"After" mean	11.9	(35)	17.0	(29)	13.0	(24)	11.7	(16)

As noted previously, several longitudinal studies do comparisons of before and after indices. These "before" and "after" mean scores indicate a net increase in friendship contact for all housing groups in the Boston sample. Nevertheless, examination of the neighboring data has suggested that making simple comparisons may lead to overlooking internal variations due to varying lengths of time in the new residence. Such would appear to be the case in regard to friendship contact, as can be seen in Figure 8:2. Figure 8:2 presents the graph of friendship contact for each of the several housing groups, again at different intervals from the date of the "move-in." The pattern, although somewhat more erratic than that of neighboring, is one of general increases. But this is reasonable. Unlike ties to neighbors, friendship ties are not necessarily locale-based. Geographical mobility, even the one-mile moves of the Boston respondents, undoubtedly increases the physical distance between the respondents and some of their friends. Increased distance, particularly if there are no convenient transportation links, does make interaction with some friends (especially those in old neighborhoods) more difficult and, at the least, more erratic. Since the transportation facilities in the areas in which the Boston respondents live are usually quite good, it is unlikely that transportation is an insuperable

FRIENDSHIP CONTACT:
CHANGE SCORES FOR FOUR BOSTON SAMPLES

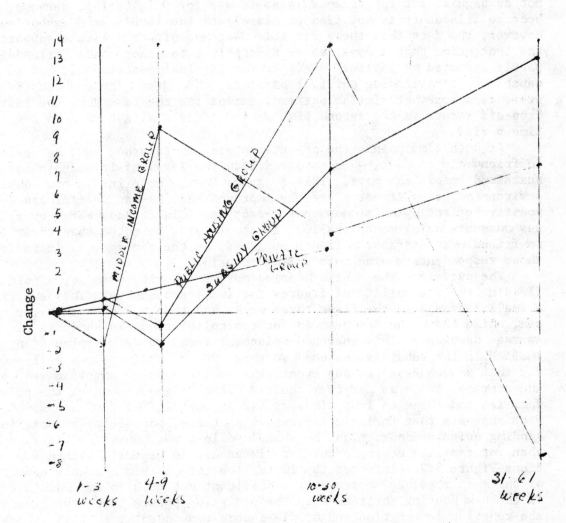

Time Elapsed Since Date of Move-in

Fig. 8:2.

problem for most friends now living a somewhat greater distance apart. In other cases the move diminishes physical distance between friends and encourages increased contact.

The middle-income group shows a slight drop-off in contact in the first few weeks after the move and an uneven but predictable rise in friendship contact above the level sustained prior to the move. The decline is not as significant for friendship as it was for neighboring, perhaps because friendship is not tied as closely to the locale as neighboring. However, the fact that there was some decrease offers a little support for the contention that a move can be disruptive; in other words, friendship is partly affected by physical distance and physical containment, but is also capable of transcending physical barriers. The graph for the subsidy sample presents a somewhat similar pattern, except for the fact that the initial drop-off occurs in the second time period after a slight rise in the first time period.

At both time points the private housing movers show some net gain in friendship contact, when compared with the level of friendship interaction sustained before the move. This suggests that a move into a new housing environment, even if not a greatly improved one, has an initial and generally positive effect upon friendship interaction. Old friends carry over; and new ones are being made locally. It should also be noted that their increase in friendship interaction is not as great, on the average, as it is for those respondents moving into 221(d)3 housing.

The curve for the public housing movers is quite erratic, a gain reflecting the instability of figures for small subsamples. They experienced a small increase in the first three weeks and then a decrease in the next six, while those who had been in for ten to thirty weeks showed a sizeable average decrease. This uneven development seems to defy explanation; the small N in the subdivisions used in this type of analysis may well account for this unevenness. In any event, the public housing sample moved, on the average, twice as far from their sending neighborhoods as the private families and three to four times as far as the 221(d)3 families moved. This fact suggests that their interpersonal contacts, particularly those in the sending neighborhoods, might be sustained in a more unsystematic fashion than for families moving a shorter distance. In general, with a few exceptions Figure 8:2 reinforces the impression gained from a simple comparison of the mean absolute scores -- a significant net gain in friendship contact in the new housing environment. The net gain appears to be the greatest for the rent supplementation and middle-income respondents, that is, those living in 221(d)3 developments the architecture of which fosters tenant contacts.

The third type of primary tie examined in earlier chapters was contact with relatives. This type of contact seems logically to be one step farther than neighboring or friendship links away from being strictly locale-based -- at least for the distances under consideration here. Previous studies of intra-urban mobility and its effect upon kin ties have been done, using a cross-sectional design in which working-class respondents in "before" and "after" areas were interviewed. For the rather long distances involved these studies have found a consistent decrease in kin contact with a move from the central area out to housing estates.[16] One piece of longitudinal evidence also suggests that the families moving out to the estates sharply curtail their relationships with relatives in the central city.[17] Contacts, primarily

because of substantially increased distance (four to twenty miles), become
fewer and less regular. On the basis of these findings, it is difficult to
predict the effect of the move on families moving, on the average, one
mile from their previous neighborhoods. Some may move closer to their relatives and some farther away.

The mean absolute scores for kin contact are tabulated in Table 8:7.
Again, it is useful to make simple comparisons of these mean scores prior
to examining the change scores for each of the subdivisions at the four
points in time after the move.

TABLE 8:7

MEAN CONTACT WITH RELATIVES

	Rent Supplemen- tation Sample		Middle- Income Sample		Public Housing Sample		Private Housing Sample	
	Score	N	Score	N	Score	N	Score	N
"Before" mean	10.3	(35)	14.7	(29)	12.3	(24)	9.4	(16)
"After" mean	9.7	(35)	14.8	(29)	9.7	(24)	11.0	(16)

The general impression which one gets from Table 8:7 is that the net change,
whether it be a decrease or an increase, is not as great as it was for
friendship contact; nor is it consistently an increase as it was for friendship contact. Figure 8:3 enables one to examine the distribution of these
increases and decreases over time.

The picture of changes in kin contact is rather different from that
of friendship ties. In Figure 8:2 there was an overall increase in friendship interaction and only a few decreases, generally in the first periods
after "move-in." In the kinship chart a pattern of initial decrease
followed by a rise or a decline predominates. The subsidy groups in the
first two quartiles experienced a significant drop-off in kin contact,
while the groups who had been in the new housing for a longer time reported
a net increase. The two private subdivisions show a slight decrease at the
first time point and a substantial increase by the second period. This
information does suggest an initial dip in kin contact during the settling-in
period followed by a net gain in subsequent weeks. The public housing group
interviewed shortly after the move also experienced a decrease in kin contact;
however, this decrease is not regained for those who have resided in the
housing for a longer time. The initial drop-off parallels that of the subsidy and private housing movers; but the failure of later groups to fully
reestablish their prior contacts jibes with the prior findings on their
friend and neighbor contacts and their general dissatisfaction with current
housing. Except for the public housing movers, no sample shows a systematic,

116

CONTACT WITH RELATIVES:
CHANGE SCORES FOR FOUR BOSTON SAMPLES

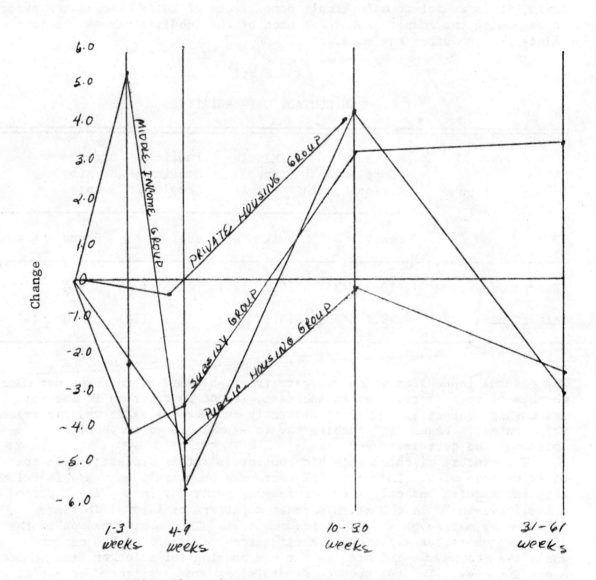

Time Elapsed Since Date of Move-in

Fig. 8:3.

lasting decrease in interaction with kin, as was predicted on the basis of the British studies. The middle-income groups present a difficult-to-interpret alternating pattern; again this points up the difficulty of doing cross-sectional comparisons of small subsamples. The relatively small number in each group leaves room for idiosyncratic variations in the contacts of a few individuals to significantly affect the mean; in fact, the kin ties of individuals are not entirely voluntary and can easily be altered by the coming and going of relatives in the Boston area.

Some additional data suggest the relative importance of these three types of primary ties during the move itself. Each respondent was asked three questions about the number of neighbors, friends, and relatives who helped her move into her new apartment (or house). The results of the questions can be seen in Table 8:8.

TABLE 8:8

PERCENT OF BOSTON SAMPLES RECEIVING AID FROM PRIMARY GROUPS

| | Number | Percent of Respondents Receiving Aid in the "Move-in" | | |
		From New Neighbors	From Friends	From Relatives
Rent supplementation sample	35	11.4%	42.9%	54.3%
Middle-income sample	29	13.8%	58.6%	58.6%
Public housing sample	24	25.0%	41.7%	50.0%
Private housing sample	16	37.5%	68.2%	18.8%

Taking all the movers together, it is evident that these Negro respondents relied much more heavily on previous friendships and on kin ties during the move-in period than they did on their new neighbors; this fits in well with the systematic decrease in neighboring which all four groups experienced during the first nine weeks after moving into their new residences. Although there was also some decrease in overall kin contact during the first few weeks after the move-in for most of the housing groups, this should not be interpreted as a loss of contact with all relatives. Some relatives were very important sources of aid in the "settling-in" process. A majority of the respondents in each of the three project groups received aid from one or more relatives. Except for the private movers no groups had a larger percentage of respondents depending on friends than depending on relatives. This importance of relatives in the process of moving corroborates a statement made in an earlier chapter about the importance of kin contacts even for this sample of relatively recent migrants to the Boston area. At least for the majority of these working-class blacks, kinship networks do as a matter of fact mobilize to help with relatively short-range geographical mobility.

As can be seen in Table 8:8, friendship ties were likewise important in easing the transition from one neighborhood to another. From 42% to 68% of each group received aid from friends in the transitional period. This too fits in well with the previously noted importance of friendship to these black Bostonians. It also corroborates the longitudinal evidence which generally indicated the strength and persistence of friendship links during the "move-in" period (Figure 8:2). Primary ties, particularly those of kinship and friendship, are probably the most important mechanisms for inte-grating working-class families, including Negro families, into an urban area. Their importance is tested in practice when a minor household crisis, such as a move, occurs.

The effect of a move on associational affiliations has been studied by few researchers. Two British cross-sectional studies conflict with one another. Marris' research revealed that Africans relocated in a new housing estate belonged to fewer clubs and associations than their central city counterparts.[18] Mogey found the opposite for his white working-class families in an Oxford housing estate, as compared with a central city sample.[19] One longitudinal study, conducted in 1939-1940 in Minneapolis, found that res-pondents who moved into an improved housing environment gained in associa-tional participation asmeasured by the Chapin participation scale.[20] This led me to predict the following long-term effect in regard to the Boston samples: there will be a positive increase in secondary participation with a relatively short-range move into an improved housing environment. None of the previous studies suggest what the initial effect of the move would be. It seems reasonable, nevertheless, to expect little initial change in secondary ties, since such ties are less locale-based than primary ties.

TABLE 8:9

MEAN ASSOCIATIONAL PARTICIPATION SCORE[a]

	Rent Supplemen-tation Sample		Middle-Income Sample		Public Housing Sample		Private Housing Sample	
	Score	N	Score	N	Score	N	Score	N
"Before" mean	2.1	(35)	3.7	(29)	2.9	(24)	0.8	(16)
"After" mean	1.4	(35)	5.0	(29)	1.7	(24)	1.3	(16)

[a]Because of omissions in "before-move" data, church participation has been excluded from "before" and "after" scores in this table and in Figure 8:4.

ASSOCIATIONAL PARTICIPATION:
CHANGE SCORES FOR FOUR BOSTON SAMPLES

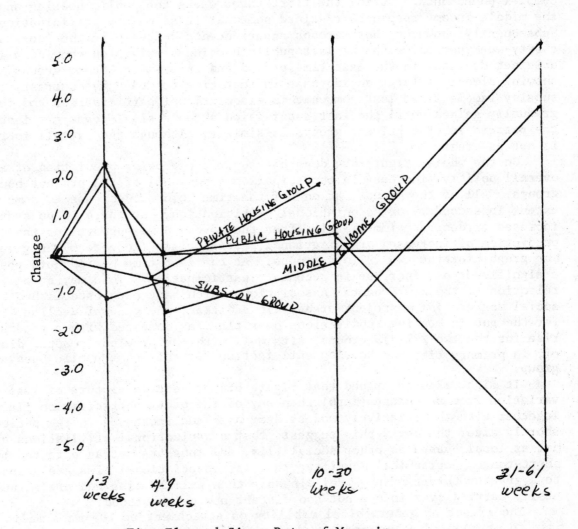

Time Elapsed Since Date of Move-in

Fig. 8:4.

Simple comparisons of "before" and "after" means for the Boston sample can be made using the data in Table 8:9. The rent supplementation and public housing samples experienced a net decrease in voluntary association participation; the middle-income and private housing groups, a net increase. However, inspection of the change scores in Figure 8:4 reveals a more complex phenomenon. During the first three weeks the public housing and the middle-income respondents gained somewhat in secondary participation. Subsequently, however, both groups experienced a decrease in the four-to-thirty-week period, with the last public housing subdivision showing a sizeable net decrease in the last time period and the middle-income groups showing almost as large an increase in that time period. By contrast, the subsidy sample first lost somewhat in associational participation and then gradually gained until the last subdivision shows a significant net increase; the pattern for the private groups is similar, although the overall increase is not as great.

On the whole, Figure 8:4 does not support the prior prediction of an overall positive increase in participation across all of the project housing groups. All of the groups, at one of the time points, decrease to some extent in secondary or associational participation, but there is no systematic increase or decrease immediately after the move. Some support for the prediction of increased organizational participation (long-term) is given by the graphs for the two 221(d)3 groups. At the last time period both posted a significant net increase in secondary participation. This may be a relection of the new Tenants' Associations which have been established by social workers in the project areas. In addition, the general decline for the public housing subdivisions over time, as compared with a general rise for the two 221(d)3 groups, fits well with the previously noted drop-off in primary ties and housing satisfaction for this same public housing group.

It might also be argued that Figure 8:4 presents a picture of less variation from no change (zero) than any of the other participation figures. Together with the relatively modest decreases and increases in the period shortly after the move, this suggests that organizational affiliations are not as locale-based as other social ties, and thus are not as affected by short-range geographical mobility; that is, associational ties are accustomed to a greater burden of physical distance than primary ties and are rather easily carried over into a not too distant new neighborhood.

The effect of geographical mobility on attachment to the mass media has, to my knowledge, never been studied. One might predict that mass media contact would increase during the first few weeks of the move and then go back to previous levels, the initial increase compensating for possible losses in friendship and neighboring interaction. Certainly the mean absolute scores, presented in Table 8:10, offer no consistent evidence for an overall loss or gain. Two groups declined slightly; the other two increased in mass media contact, although only modestly. Examination of Figure 8:5, which presents change scores for each housing group's subdivisions, reveals a relatively unsystematic relationship between mass media contact and time spent in the new housing environment. The middle-income group in the first quartile gained slightly in media contact, perhaps a partial reaction to their loss in friendship and neighboring contacts. At four to nine weeks a net decrease is indicated; this loss is recovered at the two subsequent time periods. Likewise the private housing subdivisions show a somewhat

CONTACT WITH MASS MEDIA:
CHANGE SCORES FOR FOUR BOSTON SAMPLES

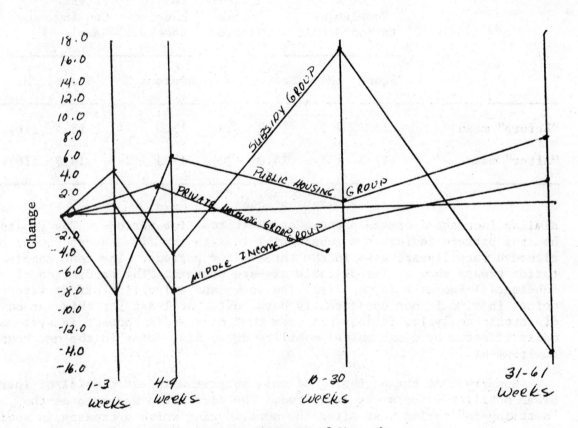

Time Elapsed Since Date of Move-in

Fig. 8:5.

TABLE 8:10

MEAN CONTACT WITH MASS MEDIA (QUARTER HOURS)

	Rent Supplemen- tation Sample		Middle- Income Sample		Public Housing Sample		Private Housing Sample	
	Score	N	Score	N	Score	N	Score	N
"Before" mean	15.7	(35)	15.2	(29)	15.0	(24)	15.4	(16)
"After" mean	17.8	(35)	15.0	(29)	17.3	(24)	14.9	(16)

similar increase-decrease pattern at their two time periods. The public housing pattern indicates a substantial loss in the first period and a net, although curvilinear, gain in the three later periods. The rent supplemen- tation groups show an inexplicable zig-zag pattern. The prediction of a substantial increase in the first few weeks and a leveling off at later points in time is not consistently borne out. At least for this method of diachronic analysis, it does not seem that mass media contact is systemati- cally affected by geographical mobility or by time spent in the new housing environment.

Summary. At the beginning of this chapter a two-step model of intra- urban mobility effects was suggested. The first step was seen as the "settling-in" period just after the move, during which decreases in social interaction are generally expected. The second step was the period of establishment of new contacts in the new housing environment.

Of the several measures of social participation used in this monograph neighboring seems to most consistently follow the steps distinguished in the model. Neighboring for all groups dropped off during the period subsequent to the move itself. Then the role of the improved housing environment, at least the greatly improved 221(d)3 environment, appears to come into play, and an increase in neighboring appears as the tenants become established in their new environment. Frienship ties were not as affected by an improved housing environment, particularly the 221(d)3 environment; the general impression is one of an increase with time in. The other measures of social participation are less systematically affected by the move and the new environment than are neighboring and friendship. Associational participation generally showed the least variation (from zero) after the move, with the private and 221(d)3 groups suggesting a dip-rise phenomenon and the public housing sample an erratic decline over time. To a certain extent kin contacts also show a dip-rise phenomenon for the subisdy and private samples, while the public housing subdivisions dipped and remained below the "before-move" level. Changes in mass media contact are perhaps the most erratic and appear to be manifesting enough idiosyncrasies to suggest that such contact is not systematically affected by the move or the new housing milieu.

In addition to looking at this model across the housing groups it is well to examine what happens to the several participation variables of any one housing group. A comparison of the figures reveals no completely systematic changes in social participation for any of the several housing groups. However, certain general impressions are gleaned from scanning the graphs. For example, the information on the public housing group does suggest that these respondents experienced increased dissatisfaction with their new housing environment over time. This dissatisfaction is reflected in (or perhaps generated by) a general decrease in their informal and formal social contacts. Neighboring and kin contacts reflect, across the time-in subdivisions, a net loss compared to "before-move" levels, as does associational participation. The only contact which showed a general rise over time was mass media contact. This certainly suggests a picture of respondents disillusioned (over time) by their new housing environment.

In striking contrast, the participation indices of the rent supplementation sample and the middle-income sample, located as they are in a substantially improved socio-physical environment, are characterized by a general rise with time in their new housing environment. The rent supplementation sample's time-in subdivisions usually reflect a dip with the move but a rise (above the "before-move" level) in informal and formal contacts at later points in time. Although somewhat more erratic, the data on the middle-income respondents present a picture similar to that for the rent supplementation sample, at least in its broad overall character. The two private housing subdivisions also approximate this picture, usually indicating some decrease with the move and a rise at the later point in time. Significantly, the rises, although generally to a point above the "before-move" level, tend to be more moderate than for the groups in 221(d)3 housing, again pointing up the socially stimulating quality of this latter type of housing.

It should be noted that this overall dip-rise effect of the move and time-in is only a general impression; almost every housing group, when examined in detail, reflects some idiosyncratic variation in regard to at least one of the participation indices. It is this latter fact which argues for considering the data only as suggestive of a dip-rise model of short-range geographical mobility into an improved housing environment; they are certainly not conclusive. This is in part due to this type of diachronic analysis. All of the graphs must be interpreted with caution, since most of the analysis of change is grounded upon comparisons of different subdivisions within each housing group rather than of the same respondents over time. This kind of analysis is in this respect cross-sectional and poses the usual problems of using synchronic data to do a diachronic analysis. However, it is more than cross-sectional since the change scores do incorporate diachronic ("after" minus "before") data and partially correct for individual variation before the move and the selectivity involved in splitting each housing group into subdivisions by length of time-in. One thing is clear: more research on these critical issues is definitely needed.

Conclusion

My survey of the effects of short-range geographical mobility upon the social ties of the Boston sample of black families is cautiously optimistic about the value of the two-step (dip-rise) model. Social participation indices were found to be affected by short-range mobility and by an improved housing environment. Additional longitudinal research on this model is definitely needed. The foregoing analysis strongly suggests that such research, in addition to studying traditional variables such as life cycle and social rank, should also examine the following factors which can affect families in migration:

1. The voluntary or involuntary character of the move;
2. The distance traversed;
3. The physical character of the new unit in relation to the last occupied unit;
4. The social character of the receiving unit; and
5. The social networks of the migrating unit.

Attention should also be paid to two categories of social effects:

1. Short-term effects: due to the potentially disruptive move itself; and
2. Long-term effects: due to the social and physical character of the new housing environment itself.

FOOTNOTES

(Chapter VIII)

[1]Marris, op. cit., pp. 153-155.

[2]Young and Willmott, op. cit., pp. 131ff. Cf. also the summary of housing estate studies in Hilda Jennings, Societies in the Making (London: Routledge and Kegan Paul, 1962), pp. 216-221.

[3]Mogey, op. cit., pp. 81ff.

[4]Marc Fried, "Grieving for a Lost Home," The Urban Condition, ed. Leonard J. Duhl (New York: Basic Books, 1963), pp. 151-171.

[5]Herbert J. Gans, "Effects of the Move from City to Suburb," The Urban Condition, ed. Leonard J. Duhl (New York: Basic Books, 1963), pp. 184-200.

[6]F. Stuart Chapin, "The Social Effects of Public Housing in Minneapolis," Sociological Research, Vol. I: A Case Approach, Matilda W. Riley (New York: Harcourt, Brace and World, 1963), pp. 603-611; and Wilner et al., op. cit., pp. 164ff. Willmott's research on an English community revealed that mobile families eventually reestablish social ties disrupted by the move; but it took many years, even a generation, for this to occur. Peter Willmott, The Evolution of a Community (London: Routledge and Kegan Paul, 1963).

[7]Officials at the Boston Housing Authority and the federal Housing and Home Finance Agency (now HUD) prefer the label of "families whose rents are supplemented" to that of "subsidy families." This chapter will use the phrases "rent supplementation families" and "subsidy families" interchangeably.

[8]Mogey, op. cit.; Marris, op. cit.; and Young and Willmott, op. cit.

[9]Wilner et al, op. cit.; Chapin, "The Social Effects of Public Housing in Minneapolis," loc. cit.

[10]Peter H. Rossi, Why Families Move (Glencoe, Illinois: Free Press, 1955).

[11]Gans, "Effects of the Move from City to Suburb," loc. cit., p. 187.

[12]Since the following analysis concentrates on this differentiation between the move and time-in, the non-movers have been omitted. Comparison of their mean absolute scores, "before" and "after," reveals little change in social participation, with two exceptions. Friendship and kinship contact do show moderate increases; this suggests even further caution in interpreting the mean absolute scores in these two areas of contact.

[13]In most cases substituting medians for means in this figure and in those following does not substantially alter the patterns over time, although it does tend to reduce the magnitude of the central tendency measure.

[14]Mogey, op. cit., pp. 94ff. Cf. also Jennings, op. cit., pp. 216ff.

[15]Berger, op. cit., p. 65.

[16]Marris, op. cit., pp. 151ff.; Mogey, op. cit., pp. 81ff,; and Jennings, op. cit., pp. 107f. Cf. also V. Hole, "Social Effects of Planned Rehousing," Town Planning Review, 30 (1959), 161-173.

[17]Young and Willmott, op. cit., pp. 131f. However, Litwak argues that the extended family has learned to minimize the disruptive effects of geographical mobility; his evidence on middle-class respondents indicates that (inter-urban) mobility has an effect on face-to-face contact but not general kin identification. Eugene Litwak, "Geographic Mobility and Extended Family Cohesion," American Sociological Review, 25 (1960), 385-394.

[18]Marris, op. cit., p. 157. Cf. also Jennings, op. cit., p.220.

[19]Mogey, op. cit., p. 113.

[20]Chapin, "The Social Effects of Public Housing in Minneapolis," loc. cit., pp. 603ff.

CHAPTER IX

SUMMARY AND CONCLUSIONS

The general neglect of social organization, particularly the more
intimate forms of social contact, within the residential communities of black
Americans suggested the need for an intensive examination of the various social
ties of a black sample in Boston. To offset the undue emphasis on social disorganization, and the general tendency to view the black ghetto as a "jungle," this
monograph has examined the extent to which black urbanites maintain interpersonal ties even within the ghetto area.

The dominant impression which one gets from examining the Boston data on
primary ties is that these black respondents definitely do not fit the sterotype
of the <u>isolated</u> ghetto dweller who has no concern for or contact with his or her
fellow residents. Overall these black women are by no means isolated from those
interpersonal ties which form important communication (construed in the broadest
sense)networks in urban subcommunities. Gemeinschaft is not dead in the Boston
ghetto. Several previously noted studies have revealed the importance of kin
attachments in working-class areas. Certainly the data on relatives for the
Roxbury area sample reveal that kin are quite important sources of close personal
ties for these black respondents. Significantly, considering that the majority
of these relatively poor families have come to Boston in the last two decades,
these respondents have an average of 2.6 relatives beyond their immediate family
in the Boston area. They usually see these relatives frequently, one or two
typically being visited (or visited with) weekly; and nearly half of them received
aid from relatives in moving into their current residences.

At the same time that they have presented far-reaching evidence on the
importance of kinship, these same working-class studies have usually neglected
other primary ties. Contact with relatives is only one important type of
interpersonal contact available to working-class families. A careful examination
of the friendship ties of these Boston wives, also predominantly working-class,
revealed that the great majority are not isolated from this type of intimate
social interaction. They average about three friends apiece, and typically they
visit with two of these friends several times a week. Neighbor relations
also are of some importance. Most of the respondents maintain speaking and
visiting relationships with a few of their neighbors; two-thirds have done some
visiting in neighbors' homes. Thus, friendship and neighboring ties are
significant components of the social lives of these respondents and are major
criteria for designating their local residential area a "neighborhood." In
addition to emphasizing the importance of interpersonal contacts for working-
class families in a black community, the above data point to the need to
systematically study friendship and neighboring ties in other blue-collar areas.

The integration of these black respondents into the social life of the urban subcommunity appears to be roughly comparable to that of working-class whites. Admittedly the variety of indices used in the various studies of social participation make it difficult to cumulate research in this area. Nevertheless, these black women have informal ties, apparently as strong (extensive and intensive) as have been found for comparable white samples. With the exception of church participation their associational ties are generally weak and broadly similar to the extent of urban white participation; and their contact with mass media roughly approximates that of blue-collar whites.

Gans' working-class Italians appear to have limited their social ties to the local West End area; it is not surprising then, especially considering omnipresent discrimination, that these black urbanites generally confine most of their important social ties to a geographically limited area. Approximately 95% of their friends and 97% of their relatives live within the general Roxbury-South End-Dorchester area. The same encapsulation was found to be true of what associational affiliations these respondents do maintain. Although the addresses of associations are not always ascertainable, those which can be plotted indicate that almost all memberships are likewise limited to the Roxbury-South End-Dorchester area. The findings on forms of urban participation involving more tenuous intersonal contacts corroborate this image of encapsulation. These black respondents make relatively few ventures beyond the ghetto for recreational reasons except for "riding around in the car for pleasure"; and a very large percentage of their commercial trips are confined to the ghetto area. In general, this encapsulation of social ties and associational non-participation jibes with a picture of black dependence.

Some variation in social participation was found within the Boston sample. Those who are more active in one type of social participation, associational contacts, also tend to maintain more active friendships and neighboring than those not so active in associations. However, no correlation turned up between informal contacts and mass media contact; there was some evidence of a threshold level of mass media contact for those who are associationally active. Participation differences due to social status have previously been found in regard to white samples. The Boston data support the contention that upper-blue-collar respondents are somewhat more active in each of the three areas of participation than lower-blue-collar respondents. In most instances the differences are not very great; one gets the impression that these two blue-collar groups might appear more similar than different if they were compared with higher status groups.

To a variable extent, relatively short-range mobility was found to effect variations in the participation measures of these black respondents. Some evidence was presented for a dip-rise model of short-range geographical mobility. Except for mass media contact there was a general tendency for participation to decline in the first few weeks after the move and to rise above previous levels with time in a new and improved housing environment. However, the results for the public housing group indicated a general decline over time, while the two 221(d)3 groups revealed the most consistent rise effect after the initial move-in period. Exceptions to the dip-rise prediction are numerous enough to make the evidence more suggestive than conclusive. In addition to pointing up the effects of mobility for black Americans, the evidence has broader implications. The dip-rise model would seem to be applicable to the study of all short-range geographical mobility. I would advocate further testing of this general hypothesis.

It is worth reemphasizing that the sample of black Bostonians is representative only of a certain segment of the population of the Roxbury area; it is most closely representative of the larger low- and middle-income families in the area. In addition, its mobility subsamples form between 70% and 90% of all large low-income and middle-income families in certain Roxbury area housing markets at the times we selected our samples. They are more representative of families who have moved relatively recently than of those who have not moved. Although a few families have moved to the fringe of the ghetto, most families moved even closer to the heart of Roxbury itself, particularly the sixty-four now residing in the 221(d)3 projects. The net effect of moving was to increase the concentration of these black families in the heart of the ghetto. All of these factors should be taken into consideration when extrapolating beyond the sample to the whole Roxbury ghetto area. Yet the data might well be used as a first approximation of interpersonal life in a black community. Of the two views of the ghetto this approximation comes closer to the "village" view than to the more usual "jungle" picture: ordinary social life does go on within the ghetto.

Moreover, the data are representative enough to suggest that public policy decisions in regard to black areas must take into consideration the ordinary and "normal" social ties which tend to bind people to their community and which probably provide major communications networks for that area. The usual reliance on formal associations and the mass media in trying to communicate with the low-income segment of the urban population is inadequate, not only because of the linguistic barrier but also because it overlooks primary networks. The explanations of the failure to reach the poor, such as in elections of the poor to "war on poverty" committees, are usually given in terms of their isolation and anomie; a more reasonable explanation may well be the policy makers' and planners' ignorance of social networks in relatively low-income areas.

This research suggests two logical and important extensions:

1. One important extension of the research on friendship and kinship interaction would be a study of the social networks moving out beyond the individual black respondent and her immediate circle of friends and relatives. Like almost all previous studies, we have investigated only the stub ends of social networks, that is, the respondent and the "first remove." The impression gained from comparing certain of the Boston study interviews is that many of these networks do spread out beyond the "first remove" into the broader black community. Whether or not this is actually the case remains to be seen; further research on urban networks is definitely a necessity.

2. A logical extension of the mobility research would parallel our original plan of a controlled study of black families in alternative housing markets with an interview before the move and several additional interviews commencing shortly after the move and repeated at regular intervals on the same respondents. Such an extension would involve the very difficult problem of intervention in real social processes. Longitudinal research of this type requires careful control of move-in dates and coordination of procedures of selection; public agencies, at least in the area of housing, are just beginning to be sensitized to the complex research procedures central to such research. However difficult and expensive it may be, longitudinal research is virtually the only way to correct for our current overdependence on cross-sectional comparisons for diachronic inferences about the effects of mobility and housing.

BIBLIOGRAPHY

Advisory Committee on Racial Imbalance and Education. Because It Is Right --
    Educationally. Massachusetts State Board of Education, 1965.

Angell, R. C. "The Moral Integration of American Cities," in Cities and
    Society. Edited by Paul K. Hatt and Albert J. Reiss, Jr. New York:
    The Free Press of Glencoe, 1957, pp. 617-630.

Atwood, B. S., and Schideler, E. H. "Social Participation and Juvenile
    Delinquency," Sociology and Social Research, 18 (1934), 436-441.

Axelrod, Morris. "Urban Structure and Social Participation," in Cities and
    Society. Edited by Paul K. Hatt and Albert J. Reiss, Jr. New York:
    The Free Press of Glencoe, 1957, pp. 722-729.

Babchuk, Nicholas. "Primary Friends and Kin: A Study of the Associations of
    Middle Class Couples," Social Forces, 43 (1964-1965), 483-493.

Babchuk, Nicholas, and Edwards, John N. "Voluntary Associations and the
    Integration Hypothesis," Sociological Inquiry, 35 (1965), 149-162.

Babchuk, Nicholas, and Gordon, C. Wayne. The Voluntary Association in the
    Slum. (University of Nebraska Studies: New Series No. 27.) Lincoln:
    University of Nebraska Press, 1962.

Babchuk, Nicholas, and Thompson, Ralph V. "The Voluntary Associations of
    Negroes," American Sociological Review, 27 (1962), 647-655.

Back, Kurt W. Slums, Projects, and People. Durham: Duke University Press,
    1962.

Barnes, J. A. "Class and Committees in a Norweigian Island Parish," Human
    Relations, 7 (1954), 39-58.

Barnland, Dean C., and Harland, Carroll. "Propinquity and Prestige as
    Determinants of Communication Networks," Sociometry, 26 (1963),
    467-479.

Bauer, E. Jackson. "Public Opinion and the Primary Group," American
    Sociological Review, 25 (1960), 208-219.

Bell, Wendell, and Boat, Marion D. "Urban Neighborhoods and Informal Social
    Relations," The American Journal of Sociology, 62 (1957), 391-398.

Berger, Bennet M. "The Myth of Suburbia," Journal of Social Issues, 17 (1961), 38-49.

_____. Working-Class Suburb. Berkeley: University of California Press, 1960.

Bernard, Jessie. "An Instrument for the Measurement of Neighborhood with Experimental Applications," Southwestern Social Science Quarterly (September, 1937), pp. 145-160.

_____. "The Neighborhood Behavior of School Children in Relation to Age and Socioeconomic Status," American Sociological Review, 4 (1939), 652-662.

Beshers, James M. Urban Social Structure. Glencoe, Illinois: The Free Press, 1962.

Blum, Alan F. "Social Structure, Social Class, and Participation in Primary Relationships," in Blue-Collar World. Edited by Arthur B. Shostak and William Gomberg. Englewood Cliffs, New Jersey: Prentice-Hall, 1964, pp. 195-207.

Blumberg, Leonard, and Bell, Robert R. "Urban Migration and Kinship Ties," Social Problems, 6 (1959), 328-333.

Bogart, Leo. "The Mass Media and the Blue-Collar Worker," in Blue-Collar World. Edited by Arthur B. Shostak and William Gomberg. Englewood Cliffs, New Jersey: Prentice-Hall, 1964, pp. 416-428.

Bott, Elizabeth. Family and Social Network. London: Tavistock Publications Limited, 1959.

Burgess, Ernest W. "Growth of the City: An Introduction to a Research Project," in Studies in Human Ecology. Edited by George A. Theodorson. New York: Harper and Row, 1961, pp. 37-44.

Burgess, M. Elaine. Negro Leadership in a Southern City. New Haven: College and University Press Paperback, 1962.

Byrne, D., and Buchler, John. "A Note on the Influence of Propinquity upon Acquaintanceships," Journal of American Social Psychology, 51 (1955), 147-148.

Caplow, Theodore, and Forman, Robert. "Neighborhood Interaction in a Homogeneous Community," American Sociological Review, 15 (1950), 357-366.

Caplow, Theodore, Stryker, Sheldon, and Wallace, Samuel E. The Urban Ambience. New York: Bedminster Press, 1964.

Chapin, F. Stuart. "The Effects of Slum Clearance and Rehousing on Family and Community Relationships in Minneapolis," American Journal of Sociology, 43 (1938), 744-763.

_____. "The Measurement of Sociability and Socio-Economic Status," *Sociology and Sociological Research*, 12 (1927-1928), 208-217.

_____. "The Relation of Sociometry to Planning in an Expanding Social Universe," *Sociometry*, 6 (1943), 234-240.

_____. "The Social Effects of Public Housing in Minneapolis," in *Sociological Research*. Vol. I: *A Case Approach*. Matilda W. Riley. New York: Harcourt, Brace and World, 1963, pp. 603-611.

_____. "Social Participation and Social Intelligence," *American Sociological Review*, 4 (1939), 157-168.

_____. "Some Housing Factors Related to Mental Hygiene," *Social Policy and Social Research in Housing*, 7 (1951), 164-171.

Christiansen, John R. "The Behavioral Correlates of Membership in Rural Neighborhoods," *Rural Sociology*, 22 (1957), 12-19.

Clark, Kenneth B. *Dark Ghetto*. New York: Harper and Row, 1965.

Clarke, Alfred C. "The Use of Leisure and Its Relation to Levels of Occupational Prestige," *American Sociological Review*, 21 (1956), 301-307.

Cohen, A. K., and Hodges, H. M. "Characteristics of the Lower-Blue-Collar-Class," *Social Problems*, 10 (1963), 303-334.

Conference on Economic Progress. *Poverty and Deprivation in the United States* (Washington, 1961).

Coult, Allan D., and Habenstein, Robert W. "The Functions of Extended Kinship in an Urban Milieu: A Comparative Study." Unpublished paper, February 28, 1961.

Davies, Vernon. "Neighborhoods, Townships, and Communities in Wright County, Minnesota," *Rural Sociology*, 9 (1943), 51-61.

Davis, Allison, Gardner, Burleigh B., and Gardner, Mary R. *Deep South*. Chicago: University of Chicago Press, 1941.

de Grazia, Sebastian. "The Uses of Time," in *Aging and Leisure*. Edited by Robert W. Kleemeier. New York: Oxford University Press, 1961, pp. 113-154.

Detroit Area Study. *A Social Profile of Detroit*. Ann Arbor: University of Michigan Press, 1952.

Dewey, Richard. "The Neighborhood, Urban Ecology, and City Planners," in *Cities and Society*. Edited by Paul K. Hatt and Albert J. Reiss, Jr. New York: The Free Press of Glencoe, 1957, pp. 783-790.

Dobiner, William M. (ed.). The Suburban Community. New York: G. P. Putnam's Sons, 1958.

Dollard, John. Caste and Class in a Southern Town. 3rd ed. Garden City: Doubleday Anchor Books, 1949.

Dotson, Floyd. "Participation in Voluntary Associations in a Mexican City," American Sociological Review, 18 (1953), 380-386.

_____. "Patterns of Voluntary Associations Among Working-Class Families," American Sociological Review, 16 (1951), 687-693.

Drake, St. Clair. "The Social and Economic Status of the Negro in the United States," Daedalus, 94 (1965), 771-814.

Drake, St. Clair, and Cayton, Horace R. Black Metropolis. Vols. I and II. New York: Harper Torchbooks, 1962.

Duhl, Leonard J. (ed.). The Urban Condition. New York: Basic Books, 1963.

Edwards, Rheable M. Morris, Laura B., and Coard, Robert M. "The Negro in Boston." Boston: Action for Boston Community Development, 1961. (Mimeographed.)

Fava, Sylvia F. "Contrasts in Neighboring: New York City and a Suburban Community," in The Suburban Community. Edited by William M. Dobriner. New York: G. P. Putnam's Sons, 1958, pp. 122-131.

Fellin, Phillip, and Litwack, Eugene. "Neighborhood Cohesion Under Conditions of Mobility," American Sociological Review, 28 (1963), 364-376.

Festinger, Leon, Schachter, Stanley, and Back, Kurt. Social Pressures in Informal Groups. New York: Harper and Row, 1950.

Foley, Donald L. "Neighbors or Urbanites?" University of Rochester, 1952, chapter 3. (Mimeographed.) Cited in Urban Society. 5th ed. Noel P. Gist and Sylvia F. Fava. New York: Thomas Y. Crowell, 1964, pp. 406-407.

_____. "The Use of Local Facilities in a Metropolis," in Cities and Society. Edited by Paul K. Hatt and Albert J. Reiss, Jr. New York: The Free Press of Glencoe, 1957, pp. 607-616.

Foote, Nelson N., et al. Housing Choices and Housing Constraints. New York: McGraw-Hill, 1960.

Form, William H. "Status Stratification in a Planned Community," in The Suburban Community. Edited by William M. Dobriner. New York: G. P. Putnam's Sons, 1958, pp. 209-224.

_____. "Stratification in Low and Middle Income Housing Areas," Social Policy and Social Research in Housing, 7 (1951), 109-131.

Frazier, E. Franklin. Black Bourgeoisie. New York: Collier Books, 1962.

_____. "The Impact of Urban Civilization Upon Negro Family Life," in Cities and Society. Edited by Paul K. Hatt and Albert J. Reiss, Jr. New York: The Free Press of Glencoe, 1957, pp. 490-499.

_____. The Negro Family in Chicago. Chicago: University of Chicago Press, 1932.

Fried, Marc. "Grieving for a Lost Home," in The Urban Condition. Edited By Leonard J. Duhl. New York: Basic Books, 1963, pp. 151-171.

Fried, Marc, and Gleicher, Peggy. "Some Sources of Residential Satisfaction in an Urban Slum," Journal of the American Institute of Planners, 27 (1961), 305-315.

Frieden, Bernard J. The Future of Old Neighborhoods. Cambridge: The M. I. T. Press, 1964.

Gans, Herbert J. "Effects of the Move from City to Suburb," in The Urban Condition. Edited by Leonard J. Duhl. New York: Basic Books, 1963, pp. 184-200.

_____. "Planning and Social Life," Journal of the American Institute of Planning, 27 (1961), 134-140.

_____. The Urban Villagers. New York: The Free Press of Glencoe, 1962.

Glazer, Nathan, and Moynihan, Daniel P. Beyond the Melting Pot. Cambridge: The M. I. T. Press and Harvard University Press, 1963.

Goldhamer, Herbert. "Voluntary Associations in the United States," in Cities and Society. Edited by Paul K. Hatt and Albert J. Reiss, Jr. New York: The Free Press of Glencoe, 1957, pp. 591-596.

Graham, Saxon. "Social Correlates of Adult Leisure-Time Behavior," in Community Structure and Analysis. Edited by Marvin B. Sussman. New York: Thomas Y. Crowell, 1959, pp. 331-354.

Greer, Scott. The Emerging City. New York: The Free Press of Glencoe, 1962.

Greer, Scott, and Kube, Ella. "Urbanism and Social Structure: A Los Angeles Study," in Community Structure and Analysis, Edited by Marvin B. Sussman. New York: Thomas Y. Crowell, 1959, pp. 93-112.

Gullahorn, John. "Distance and Friendship as Factors in the Gross Interaction Matrix," Sociometry, 15 (1952), 123-134.

Hamilton, Richard. "The Behavior and Values of Skilled Workers," in Blue-Collar World. Edited by Arthur Shostak and William Gomberg. Englewood Cliffs, New Jersey: Prentice-Hall, 1964, pp. 42-57.

Handel, Gerald, and Rainwater, Lee. "Persistence and Change in Working-Class Life Style," Sociology and Social Research, 48 (1964), 281-288.

Harrington, Michael. The Other America. New York: The Macmillan Company, 1962.

Hauser, Philip M. "On the Impact of Urbanism on Social Organization, Human Nature and the Political Order," Confluence, 7 (1958), 57-69.

Hausknecht, Murray. The Joiners. New York: Bedminster Press, 1962.

Hay, Donald G. "A Scale for Measurement of Social Participation of Rural Households," Rural Sociology, 13 (1948), 285-294.

Heberle, Rudolf. "The Normative Element in Neighborhood Relations," The Pacific Sociological Review, 3 (1960), 3-11.

Hill, Adelaide. "The Negro Upper Class in Boston, Its Development and Present Social Structure." Unpublished Ph.D. thesis, Radcliffe College, 1952.

Hoggart, Richard. The Uses of Literacy. Boston: Beacon Paperback, 1961.

Hole, V. "Social Effects of Planned Rehousing," Town Planning Review, 30 (1959), 161-173.

Horton, Donald, and Strauss, Anselm. "Interaction in Audience-Participation Shows," American Journal of Sociology, 62 (1957), 579-587.

Horton, Donald and Wohl, R. R. "Mass Media and Para-Social Interaction," Psychiatry, 3 (1956), 215-299.

Housing and Home Finance Agency. Low-Income Housing Demonstration. Washington: Government Printing Office, 1964.

Hunter, Floyd. Community Power Structure. Chapel Hill: The University of North Carolina Press, 1953.

Hypes, J. L. Social Participation in a Rural New England Town. New York: Columbia University Press, 1927.

Jacobs, Jane. The Death and Life of Great American Cities. New York: Vintage Books, 1961.

Janowitz, Morris. The Community Press in an Urban Setting. Glencoe, Illinois: The Free Press, 1952.

Jennings, Hilda. Societies in the Making. London: Routledge and Paul, 1962.

Jones, Thomas J. The Sociology of a New York City Block. New York: Columbia University Press, 1904.

Katz, Elihu, and Lazarsfeld, Paul F. Personal Influence. New York: Free Press Paperback, 1964.

Kerr, Madeline. The People of Ship Street. London: Routledge and Kegan Paul, 1958.

Key, William H. "Rural-Urban Differences and the Family," The Sociological Quarterly, 2 (1961), 49-56.

Kiser, Clyde V. Sea Island to City: A Study of St. Helena Islanders in Harlem and Other Urban Centers. New York: Columbia University Press, 1952.

Knupfer, Genevieve. "Portrait of the Underdog," in Class, Status and Power. Edited by Reinhard Bendix and Seymour M. Lipset. Glencoe, Illinois: The Free Press, 1953, pp. 255-263.

Komarovsky, Mirra. Blue-Collar Marriage. New York: Random House, 1962.

_____. "The Voluntary Associations of Urban Dwellers," American Sociological Review, 11 (1946), 686-698.

Kornhauser, William. The Politics of Mass Society. Glencoe, Illinois: The Free Press, 1959.

Kriesberg, Louis, and Bellin, Seymour S. "The World of Informal Social Relations: Neighbors, Friends and Kinsmen," in Fatherless Families and Housing: A Study of Dependency. Louis Kriesberg and Seymour S. Bellin. Syracuse, New York: Syracuse University and Youth Development Center, 1965, pp. 157-208.

Lampman, Robert J. "The Low Income Population and Economic Growth," Joint Economic Committee (Congress) Study Paper No. 12. Washington: Government Printing Office, 1959.

Landecker, Werner S. "Types of Integration and their Measurement," American Journal of Sociology, 56 (1951), 332-340.

Lazarsfeld, Paul F., and Merton, Robert K. "Friendship as Social Process: A Substantive and Methodological Analysis," in Sociological Research: Vol. I: A Case Approach. Matilda W. Riley. New York: Harcourt, Brace and World, 1963, pp. 513-530.

Lee, Frank F. Negro and White in Connecticut Town. New Haven: College and University Press Paperback, 1961.

Le Play, F. Les Ouvriers Europeens. Paris, 1877.

Lewis, Hylan. Blackways of Kent. New Haven: College and University Press Paperback, 1964.

Lionberger, Hubert F., and Hassinger, Edward. "Neighborhoods as a Factor in the Diffusion of Farm Information in a Northeast Missouri Farming Community," Rural Sociology, 19 (1954), 377-384.

Litwak, Eugene. "Geographic Mobility and Extended Family Cohesion," American Sociological Review, 25 (1960), 385-394.

_____. "Occupational Mobility and Extended Family Cohesion," American Sociological Review, 25 (1960), 9-21.

Lundberg, George A., and Lawsing, Margaret. "The Sociograph of Some Community Relations," in Sociological Research. Vol. I: A Case Approach. Matilda W. Riley. New York: Harcourt, Brace and World, 1963, pp. 141-152.

Lundberg, George A., and Steele, M. "Social Attraction Patterns in a Village," Sociometry, 1 (1938), 375-419.

Lynd, Robert, and Lynd, Helen. Middletown. New York: Harcourt-Brace and Co., 1929.

Marcuse, Herbert. One-Dimensional Man. Boston: Beacon Press, 1964.

Marris, Peter. Family and Social Change in an African City. Chicago: Northwestern University Press, 1962.

McEntire, Davis. Residence and Race. Berkeley: University of California Press, 1960.

McKenzie, R. D. "The Neighborhood: A Study of Local Life in the City of Columbus, Ohio," American Journal of Sociology, 27 (1922), 486-509.

Meadow, Kathryn P. "Negro-White Differences Among Newcomers to a Transitional Urban Area," The Journal of Intergroup Relations, 3 (1962), 320-330.

Merton, Robert K. "Patterns of Influence: A Study of Interpersonal Influence and of Communications Behavior in a Local Community," in Sociological Research: Vol. I. A Case Approach. Matilda W. Riley. New York: Harcourt, Brace and World, 1963, pp. 153-165.

_____. "The Social Psychology of Housing," in Current Trends in Social Psychology. Edited by W. Dennis. Pittsburgh: University of Pittsburgh Press, 1948.

Meyersohn, Rolf. "A Critical Examination of Commercial Entertainment," in Aging and Leisure. Edited by Robert W. Kleemeier. New York: Oxford University Press, 1961, pp. 243-272.

Michel, Andree V. "Kinship Relations and Relationships of Proximity in French Working-class Households," in A Modern Introduction to the Family. Edited by N. W. Bell and E. F. Vogel. Glencoe, Illinois: The Free Press, 1960, pp. 287-294.

Miller, S. M. "The American Lower Classes: A Typological Approach," in Blue-Collar World. Edited by Arthur B. Shostak and William Gomberg. Englewood Cliffs, New Jersey: Prentice-Hall, 1964, pp. 9-23.

_____. "The 'New' Working Class," in Blue-Collar World. Edited by Arthur B. Shostak and William Gomberg. Englewood Cliffs, New Jersey: Prentice-Hall, 1964, pp. 2-9.

Millspaugh, Martin, and Breckenfeld, Gurney. The Human Side of Urban Renewal. New York: Ives Washburn, Inc., 1960.

Minnis, Mhyra S. "The Patterns of Women's Organizations: Significance, Types, Social Prestige Rank, and Activities," in Community Structure and Analysis. Edited by Marvin B. Sussman. New York: Thomas Y. Crowell Company, 1959, pp. 269-287.

Mogey, J. M. Family and Neighborhood. London: Oxford University Press, 1956.

Myrdal, Gunnar. An American Dilemma. Vol. II. New York: McGraw-Hill Paperback, 1964.

Nisbet, Robert A. Community and Power. New York: Oxford University Press, 1962.

North, C. C. Social Differentiation. Chapel Hill: University of North Carolina Press, 1927.

Oeser, O. A., and Hammond, S. B. (eds.). Social Structure and Personality in a City. London: Routledge and Kegan Paul, 1954.

Office of Policy Planning and Research, United States Department of Labor. The Negro Family. Washington: Government Printing Office, 1965.

Padilla, Elena. Up from Puerto Rico. New York: Columbia University Press, 1958.

Parsons, Talcott. Essays in Sociological Theory. Rev. ed. Glencoe, Illinois: The Free Press, 1954.

Parsons, Talcott, and Bales, Robert. Family, Socialization and Interaction Process. Glencoe, Illinois: The Free Press, 1955.

Pettigrew, Thomas F. "Metropolitan Boston's Race Problem in Perspective," in Social Structure and Human Problems in the Boston Metropolitan Area. Metropolitan Area Planning Council, Commonwealth of Massachusetts. Cambridge: Joint Center for Urban Studies, 1965, pp. 33-51.

_____. A Profile of the Negro American. Princeton: D. Van Nostrand Company, 1964.

Pettigrew, Thomas F., and Pajonas, Patricia. "Social Psychological Considerations of Racially-Balanced Schools," in Because It is Right -- Educationally. Advisory Committee on Racial Imbalance in Education. Massachusetts State Board of Education, 1965, pp. 87-108.

Powdermaker, Hortense. After Freedom: A Cultural Study in the Deep South. New York: The Viking Press, 1939.

_____. Copper Town: Changing Africa. New York: Harper Colophon Books, 1962.

Queen, Stuart A. "Social Participation in Relation to Social Disorganization," American Sociological Review, 14 (1949), 251-257.

Rainwater, Lee. "Crucible of Identity: The Negro Lower-Class Family," Daedalus, 95 (1966), 172-216.

Rapkin, Chester, and Grigsby, William G. The Demand for Housing in Racially Mixed Areas. Berkeley: University of California Press, 1960.

Reiss, Albert J., Jr. "Rural-Urban and Status Differences in Inter-personal Contacts," American Jouranl of Sociology, 65 (1959), 182-195.

Riemer, Svend. "Urban Personality -- Reconsidered," in Community Structure and Analysis. Edited by Marvin B. Sussman. New York: Thomas Y. Crowell, 1959, pp. 433-444.

Riemer, Svend, and McNamara, John. "Contact Patterns in the City," Social Forces, 36 (1957), 137-141.

Riley, Matilda W., and Riley, John W., Jr. "A Sociological Approach to Community Research," Public Opinion Quarterly, 15 (1951), 445-460.

Rodman, Hyman. "On Understanding Lower-Class Behaviour," Social and Economic Studies, 8 (1959), 441-450.

Rose, Arnold. "Attitudinal Correlates of Social Participation," Social Forces, 37 (1959), 202-206.

Rosow, Irving. "The Social Effects of the Physical Environment," Journal of the American Institute of Planning, 27 (1961), 127-133.

Rossi, Peter H. Why Families Move. Glencoe, Illinois: The Free Press, 1955.

Rubin, Morton. "Negro Migration and Adjustment in Boston." Unpublished manuscript, Northeastern University, 1963.

Rumney, Jay, and Shuman, Sara. A Study of the Social Effects of Public Housing in Newark, N. J. Newark: Newark Housing Authority, 1944.

Safa, Helen Icken. "The Female-Based Household in Public Housing: A Case Study in Puerto Rico," Human Organization, 24 (1965), 135-139.

Schorr, Alvin L. Slums and Social Insecurity. Washington: Government Printing Office, n.d.

Scott, John, Jr. "Membership and Participation in Voluntary Associations," American Sociological Review, 22 (1957), 315-326.

Seeley, J. R., Sim, R. A., and Loosley, E. W. Crestwood Heights. New York: Wiley Science Editions, 1963.

Sharp, Harry, and Axelrod, Morris. "Mutual Aid Among Relatives in an Urban Population," in Principles of Sociology. Revised edition. Edited by R. Freedman et al. New York: Holt, Rhinehart, and Winston, 1952, pp. 433-439.

Shaw, C. R. Delinquency Areas. Chicago: University of Chicago Press, 1929.

Shostak, Arthur B., and Gomberg, William (eds.). Blue-Collar World. Englewood Cliffs, New Jersey: Prentice-Hall, 1964.

Shuval, Judith T. "Class and Ethnic Correlates of Casual Neighboring," American Sociological Review, 21 (1956), 453-458.

Smith, Joel, Form, William H., and Stone, Gregory P. "Local Intimacy in a Middle-Sized City," American Journal of Sociology, 60 (1954), 276-284.

Stein, Maurice R. The Eclipse of Community. New York: Harper Torchbook, 1964.

Steiner, Gary. The People Look at Television. New York: Alfred A. Knopf, 1963.

Sussman, Marvin B. (ed.). Community Structure and Analysis. New York: Thomas Y. Crowell, 1959.

_____. "The Help Pattern in the Middle Class Family," American Sociological Review, 18 (1953), 22-28.

Sussman, Marvin B., and Burchinal, Lee. "Kin Family Network: Unheralded Structure in Current Conceptualizations of Family Functioning," Marriage and Family Living, 24 (1962), 231-240.

Sussman, Marvin B., and Slater, Sherwood B. "A Reappraisal of Urban Kin Networks: Empirical Evidence," Paper given at the 58th Annual Meeting of the American Sociological Association, Los Angeles, California, August 28, 1963.

Sutcliffe, J. P., and Crabbe, B. D. "Incidence and Degrees of Friendship in Urban and Rural Areas," Social Forces, 42 (1963), 60-67.

Sweetzer, Frank L., Jr. "Home Television and Behavior: Some Tentative Conclusions," Public Opinion Quarterly, 19 (1955), 79-84.

_____. "A New Emphasis for Neighborhood Research," American Sociological Review, 7 (1942), 525-533.

Tannebaum, J. "The Neighborhood: A Socio-Psychological Analysis," Journal of Land Economics, 24 (1948), 358-369.

Thompson, Daniel C. The Negro Leadership Class. Englewood Cliffs, New Jersey: Prentice-Hall Spectrum Books, 1963.

Tilly, Charles. "Metropolitan Boston's Social Structure," in Social Structure and Human Problems in the Boston Metropolitan Area. Metropolitan Area Planning Council, Commonwealth of Massachusetts. Cambridge: Joint Center for Urban Studies, 1965, pp. 1-31.

_____. Migration to an American City. Wilmington, Delaware: Division of Urban Affairs, University of Delaware, 1965.

Tilly, Charles, and Brown, C. Harold. "On Uprooting, Kinship, and the Auspices of Migration." Unpublished paper, Joint Center for Urban Studies of the Massachusetts Institute of Technology and Harvard University, Cambridge, Massachusetts, 1964.

U.S. Bureau of the Census. U.S. Censuses of Population and Housing: 1960. Census Tracts: Boston, Mass. Final Report PHC(1)-18. Washington: Government Printing Office, 1962.

Wallin, Paul. "A Guttman Scale for Measuring Women's Neighborliness," American Journal of Sociology, 59 (1953), 241-246.

Warner, Sam B., Jr. Streetcar Suburbs. Cambridge: Harvard University Press and the M.I.T. Press, 1962.

Watts, Lewis G., et al. The Middle-Income Negro Family Faces Urban Renewal.

Weaver, R. C. The Negro Ghetto. New York: Harcourt, Brace and Co., 1948.

White, R. Clyde. "Social Class Differences in the Uses of Leisure," in Mass Leisure. Edited by Eric Larrabee and Rolf Meyersohn. Glencoe, Illinois: The Free Press, 1958, pp. 198-205.

Whyte, William F. "Social Organization in the Slums," American Sociological Review, 8 (1943), 34-39.

_____. Street Corner Society. 2d ed. Chicago: University of Chicago Press, 1955.

Whyte, William H., Jr. The Organization Man. Garden City: Doubleday Anchor Books, 1956.

Williams, James H. "Close Friendship Relations of Housewives Residing in an Urban Community," Social Forces, 36 (1958), 358-362.

Willmott, Peter. The Evolution of a Community. London: Routledge and Kegan Paul, 1963.

Wilner, Daniel M., et al. The Housing Environment and Family Life. Baltimore: The Johns Hopkins Press, 1962.

Wilner, Daniel M., Walkley, Rosabelle P., and Cook, Stuart W. Human Relations in Interracial Housing. Minneapolis: University of Minnesota Press, 1955.

Wirth, Louis. The Ghetto. Chicago: University of Chicago Press, 1928.

_____. "Urbanism as a Way of Life," American Journal of Sociology, 44 (1938), 1-24.

Woods, Robert A., and Kennedy, Albert J. The Zone of Emergence. Abridged and edited with a preface by Sam B. Warner, Jr. Cambridge: Harvard University Press, 1962.

228

Wright, Charles R., and Hyman, Herbert H. "Voluntary Association Memberships
    of American Adults: Evidence from National Sample Surveys," American
    Sociological Review, 23 (1958), 284-294.

Young, Michael, and Willmott, Peter. Family and Kinship in East London.
    Baltimore: Penguin Books, 1957.

Zimmer, Basil G. "Participation of Migration in Urban Structures," in
    Cities and Society. Edited by Paul K. Hatt and Albert J. Reiss, Jr.
    New York: The Free Press of Glencoe, 1957, pp. 730-738.

Zimmer, Basil G. and Hawley, A. H. "The Significance of Membership in
    Associations," American Journal of Sociology, 55 (1959), 196-201.

Zorbaugh, H.W. The Gold Coast and the Slum. Chicago: University of Chicago
    Press, 1929.